The 7th Destination

The 7ᵗʰ Destination

A journey unfolding the law of
Seventy times Seven

Benazir Patil

PARTRIDGE
A Penguin Random House Company

To order additional copies of this book, contact
Partridge India
000 800 10062 62
www.partridgepublishing.com/india
orders.india@partridgepublishing.com

To my Mother,

Abida Parveen Kadri

July 7, 1995, the battle for life had begun. Those moments of dejection are as fresh as ever in my memory. It is true for all; with me it definitely was: till the time one remains unexposed to the most miserable circumstances one does not understand the meaning of happiness. But I had grown up believing firmly that every emotion within had a lot to do with my own personality. I decided to combat the misery, and while doing so, I emerged as a person different from what I had known myself to be in the years before that.

June 4, 1996, the battle ended abruptly and I was left to decide, but by then I had lost myself, I could choose nothing and so 'Rejuvenation' was His decision for me. All along these years I continued to search for the strength my mom had talked of, until the day when I discovered it with me. A series of mental conversations with her finally helped in reviving all that lay inside me. The imaginations and realities expressed in this book are simply a depiction of these conversations.

Acknowledgement

While I was writing this book, I often remained with myself. In such times, I must say, a few of my loved ones gave me the much needed strength and encouragement. It is a pleasure to extend to them petals of my gratitude.

First, to my father Khalid and my mother Parveen for constantly extending their unconditional love; to my husband Deepak for being there at moments I needed him the most; and to my son Roshan, who ungrudgingly transferred my thoughts to paper at all odd hours and whenever I just wanted him to.

Among my friends, my earnest thanks go to Ashish who always responded and added value to all the weird thoughts that arose in my mind; to Neetu and Satvir I will always be indebted for listening to my deepest feelings and connections that I shared with my mom.

I thank Dr. Bhawani Shankar Tripathy for his guidance on the finer nuances of the English Language. While allowing me the much deserved poetic license, he painstakingly worked on my manuscript consistently stressing that the most complex thoughts must be expressed effectively only by the most simple words.

Prologue

The birds wondered what gift they should ask for from the *Simorgh*.

Hoopoe guided them, "Make one request; seek only Him, of all things He is best; if you're aware of Him, in all the earth, what could you wish for of a greater worth?"

Then the birds questioned about the length of journey.

"Before we reach our goal, the journey's seven valleys lie ahead," responded Hoopoe.

The birds got curious and asked how he knew about the seven valleys.

"Solomon has glanced at me," said Hoopoe.

And then Hoopoe explained to them what these seven valleys were:

> The valley of the quest filled with difficulties and trials;
> The valley of love that has nothing to do with reason;
> The valley of understanding where you overcome faults and weaknesses;
> The valley of detachment where you neither have a desire to possess nor a wish to discover;
> The valley of unity where you lose yourself in the divine essence;
> The valley of astonishment, where you forget all and forget yourself;

The last one is the valley of deprivation and death, impossible to describe, where the individual self does not exist, the present world and the future world dissolve into a great ocean.

I had read this in the *Ketaab-e-Hayaat*. But even before I read and understood it, Zeba was certainly the last word for me. It was only gradually I gathered that I was to decipher very many mysteries, my unpretentious mind certainly waited for it. Proclamations, scriptures and messages were His known ways of showing the path. But, I was fortunate to have been blessed with the wisdom of a few more.

Having left me in the refuge of Mother Earth, both Zeba and Daniyaal had departed in my most determining years. Apart from her the *Ketaab-e-Hayaat* was my only companion. Lamenting or rejoicing over things was not in my nature, I assumed, how could I be an exception in this ephemeral journey of humanity. Pain arrived, often hand in glove with pleasure, yet, what I eventually cherished was a different story. Nonetheless, nothing was untruth; my *parwaaz*, the imaginary flight took me into a realm of my own. A realm that soared me into a creation, filled with unusual lives, of lives that became the messengers of my world.

The seven occasions that Daniyaal mentioned pushed me further to comprehend what Mother Earth had to say about it. She enlightened me with the truth of transience and the strength of seventy times seven.

"Destiny has its own intentions," Nafisa Bee had reiterated. The unforgettable moments with Shivani were a part of the same design. Each of those, afresh and alive, embodied a bond I entwined myself with. Despite all my meditations, my journey from the Alvands to the seventh destination was unstoppable. A voyage, clearly undefined but somewhat determined had only emerged out of the longing to explore the obvious.

Benazir Patil

The truth that life's various facets were nothing but threads of intricately woven destiny kept on appearing over and over again. The definiteness of this feeling baffled me. My confrontation with Ayesha was yet another bewilderment of the eternity.

I had no choice; the almighty had made His decisions. Long years ago, He had created me in His own image and on the seventh day He had gifted me the whole universe. His most unwavering determination was to pour all His attributes into me, for me to understand the power of seventy times seven.

The world was built with seven divine attributes. Kindness, Severity, Harmony, Perseverance, Splendor, Attachment and Royalty: accordingly, the entire creation is a reflection of these seven attributes

Jewish mysticism

1

I arose and kissed the sun. That morning was as different as all the mornings of the past. Gazing at the shimmering sky just when I was being caressed by the cool breeze was an experience I loved more than any delicious feast.

I had reached the land I had envisioned for the last fourteen years. What could have been different about that place? The same muddy earth lay below my feet, the trees waving, the sparrows and the pigeons with watchful eyes, all familiar, resonated with the feeling of having been there before. Feeling completely welcomed, I forgot about the anguish that lay buried deep inside. By all conventional measures, I was an alien to that land, my appearance deceptive in many ways; I had nothing at all to tell anyone why I was there.

Memories flooded my mind. I had heard that memories of childhood stay longer and fresh; of youth, it is a combination of heartrending ones and happy ones. When one grows old, the memory lapses, what remains fresh is not what you thought of moments ago but what you had told your beloved years ago when you first met. The memories of last seven years seemed fresher than the ones I had lived with in the last seven days. All these years, I had thought of myself as a born traveler, but suddenly something had changed; my heart had conferred this declaration that I was nearing my destiny. Settling down in one place was neither my psyche nor my need. That way I was unusual among the contemporaries but akin to the caveman. After leaving Hamadan, I had just walked and walked, even if I halted for some time, I soon resumed the act of exploring the world.

Life, for me, had been a fusion of two streams; I celebrated it, just the way *Zarthosht* had asked of us; at other times I left no stone unturned to find the middle path the Buddha had talked about. I earned a living by working for people from all walks of life. Their lives looked appealing to me, but not in a way I would choose for myself. And so was here, to live yet another span, indubitably distinct from all the yesteryears.

There was something poignant in my entire being; my search for God was over.

I sat still on the wooden bench and waited for the souls to come around and guide me. I was to visit someone who was dead and bygone centuries ago. I was no exception though; many of them arrived here for reasons unknown, the known ones were for peace and fulfillment. The thought and sight of people doing this always lit my face with a smile. I had read about the places where people lived to seek solace from their tribulations; life had not yet taken me there—I wondered if I needed no healing—but wondered equally about not playing the role of a healer. Despite all the vague notions of all the places I had known, my keenness to visit this town knew no bounds. Guided by the seven principles that the *Ketaab-e-Hayaat* had revealed, the most fervent to me was about connectivity. So it was with the places. I had no clue if I was here to fill my mind with some comfort or there existed a connection that took me there. I had asked this to myself often, but I could not dwell on it long, precisely because I lived by my heart.

The breeze fell silent soon after the train left the station. I was the only one to alight here, as if the train ran just to bring me to this town. Fatehpur was a small town, two hundred miles away from Delhi, but closer to where stood one of the Seven Wonders of the World peacefully watching over all the happenings. The serenity of the unseen monument was seemingly floating around me.

A city dweller accustomed to the cacophony of Delhi could well have described the quietness of this town as eerie. But I was at home here. After all, I had walked the quiet world across mountains, valleys and deserts, and had mastered the language of silence. The environs spoke to me in the language I knew, and we understood each other well enough. That was not so about my language with humans; after Persian in school, I had progressed to learning Dari and Urdu. Hindi did not turn out to be very different either, but it was not a language that I had worked on, and sometimes failed to come up with the right words when I most needed it. But for last twenty one years, apprehension of not being able to speak a language of the land had never scratched my psyche; life had taught me the language of humanity and it was possible to converse with everyone in that language. I had spoken it so often through my eyes, perhaps this was why I was here.

———◈———

Shortly, I began to feel a stirring of emotions that I had never known before, the fragrance of the place was pulling me in communion with nature. I breathed in the simplicity around and felt as if my mind was getting polished—like a crystal it reflected everything that was present in my soul.

My thoughts were broken by a mild murmur of words mixed with little musical notes made by bangles. I turned to look, but unaware of my existence, two saree-clad women continued walking in their own stride. Perhaps they were used to seeing no one at the station at that hour. I vaguely knew the direction, someone in Delhi had explained to me. I made no attempts to start, however; I waited for someone to come, and often enjoyed the display of hesitation. With a pleasant motive of conversing, I longed to be accompanied, and I thought of giving some time to nature to know me. The wait for the morning to grow into its glory was worth it, I saw two men walking up to me as if they knew who I was.

"Are you a guest at someone's house here?" one of them approached me with a little smile. Their question was an evidence of my dissimilar appearance.

"Not a guest, I have come to live here," I responded. My spoken Urdu with a loaded Persian accent was slightly uncomforting for them. But, my smile hit them much more than my words. Their minds decided to ask me further and the gesture of help was in the waking.

"Any idea, where you intend to go?" the other one asked

"To the Shrine."

They offered to drop me on the way in their bullock cart; they seemed to be going to their field and were seasoned farmers. After hearing about my destination, their expressions had changed; they perhaps questioned their minds if I was just a tourist or a vagabond who would hang around the place for no reason.

"Have you been to the Shrine?" I asked them.

"We have been there just once," they responded unequivocally with a returning smile.

Despite my looks and appearances, they had really been nice, like many other people that I had met in Delhi. My vibrations of wanting to be with them as one of them had reached them easily. I had very often met such people in the past too; perhaps that was an idiosyncrasy that people possessed universally.

The town was gradually waking up to my presence: the noises of animals, the excitement of school going children, women carrying water pots added to the hustle-bustle all the more. Some of them observed me ardently, some wanted to talk, but the cart was a little faster for them to compete. I almost wanted to get down and walk with the children. They looked amused by my smile, which had broadened after seeing them. I will be able to spend time with them later; I consoled myself.

It had taken me fourteen years to reach Fatehpur. Having lived in six different destinations; this was the seventh, the last, I thought. A desire to reach here had its own reasons, barely having any semblance with the plans that travelers ever made in antiquity.

Just when my discussions with my inner self were on, I heard one of my recent companions' voice.

"Here, you have reached; it is about two miles from the station and about one mile ahead is the market place," he said.

Sufficiently happy with the information they shared and the hospitality they rendered to me, my will wished to do something for them as well. I decided to wait for the right time. While climbing down from the cart, I thanked them for their niceness and stood at the gate with a feeling of wonder. Waiting for someone to come and take cognizance of the stranger in me had become a habit over the years.

I had recently come to know more about this place from a frail old man in Delhi. With an increasing sense of curiosity, I had tried hard to find out more but was unable to get much information until I met Amrita, a teacher in one of the schools in Fatehpur who had come to Delhi for some of her work. Strangely, I didn't need to know anyone to visit this place was her response to my questions filled with anxiety. This setting-in of anxiety was indeed a phenomenon I was unaware of.

My mind instantly lingered on the seven valleys about which I had read in *Ketaab-e-Hayaat*. Though it said that one was to live longer in the valley of search and the feat of plunging into the other six valleys was to be a rather fulfilling experience, for many years I had been living happily in the valley of wonderment. Often I wished my existence ended in this one. I collided with numerous mysteries of life only to find that the almighty bestowed on me the privilege of His presence, for disclosure of every new mystery pushed me further into awe of his creations.

"Have you come to find someone?" an unknown voice enquired. I was immediately shaken by my oblivious state, he had been kind enough to ask me like this, but my answer disappointed him.

"No," I said.

"To meet someone?" he further asked emphatically.

His questions were valid. This time he understood my "no" easily. He asked me nothing after that. Just a caring look that compelled me enough to extend a broad smile and that compensated for all my refusals.

Benazir Patil

2

"Prophet Suleiman, in response to his special prayer to God was granted Kingdom and was given power over the forces of nature, devils, human beings and all other living creatures. He was also gifted with knowledge of their language and could easily communicate with them," said Zeba, the magnanimous story-teller. Her stories astonished me. I wanted to hear them again, and again, to keep them afresh in my memory.

"Once he was sitting on the side of a lake, deeply engrossed in the beauties of nature around. Suddenly his attention was drawn towards an ant creeping forward with a grain of wheat in its mouth. As it reached near the water a tortoise came out, opened its mouth, and the ant crept into it. The tortoise, closing its mouth, disappeared under water. After a while, the tortoise again sprung out of the water and standing on the lakeside opened its mouth. The Ant came out. But this time it had no grain of wheat in its mouth." she continued.

"How is that possible, Zeba? You mean the tortoise ate the ant and then released the ant again? Was it out of sympathy or was the ant crying in the stomach of the tortoise?" I asked her. I had got interested in the story after hearing this strange act of the tortoise. I thought perhaps the tortoise was like me, when it realized that the ant was crying, it let the ant go off.

"Khuda! Just like you, even Prophet Suleiman became anxious to know what had been happening under water. Since he could understand the language of all living beings, he enquired with the ant about what had happened. The ant explained that at the bottom of the lake was a stone and underneath it lived a blind ant. God had created it there, and because of blindness it could not move about. The ant continued to explain that it was appointed by God to provide daily food for the blind ant and it did this with the assistance of the tortoise. So it performed this duty for the blind ant every day," explained Zeba

"So much of goodness in the ant," I exclaimed!

"Yes," Zeba replied.

"Stories, such as these are meant to be like mirrors of truth for us. People hear the words from the mirrors but remain ignorant of these messages and their universal significance. We all know that one day God will place in our hands our books of greed and generosity, of sin and piety, and of all the good and the bad deeds that we have practised."

Zeba often told me about our interface with the truths and realities of life, emphasizing what we give to the world comes back to us. Some of these often caught my interest, and I asked her a series of questions one after the other.

For me, the story of Prophet Suleiman was not about the good deed of the helper ant, it resonated with the meticulousness of running of this cosmos, and its realm had beings that had the roles of giving and receiving. Every being had a purpose and likewise every being was provided with the care that was necessary. The story revealed to me much more than what Zeba had expected me to understand.

Zeba, a cosmic boon, was playing a distinct role in my life. Rarely had I met someone so capacitated with this ability of recognizing the givers in their lives and found that it is even rarer to find someone with the ability of giving. The stories she narrated not only coloured my life with wonderful hues but had also set my mind rippling with myriad thoughts and analysis.

Benazir Patil

After having lived in Lalejin for two years, we had shifted back to my birthplace, the city of Hamadan. Hamadan was a big town. For many days I remained overwhelmed by whatever I would see when I went with Zeba. Especially in the market place, I saw things I had never seen before, fruits I had never eaten. I was also amazed to see numerous mosques in and around the city. Life was much different with a few additional friends than before. Barely seven years old, I was learning intensely the importance of different relationships.

One day, I remained hidden in one corner. Zeba had been calling for me for quite some time. The chilly winds coming from the Alvand had added more grief to my gloomy state. For the first time I felt the coldness of the winters; before that the winters had been pretty much bearable for both Zeba and me, the snowfall was about to start perhaps.

Zeba called for me again, but I did not respond. She looked for me in the corner of the window, the place I always took refuge when I was not in the best of my moods. After seeing me quietly sobbing, she gracefully wiped my half fallen tears, caressed me and asked:

"What in the world has caused so much grief to my sweet little boy?"

"Rustom took away my toy?" said I with some added tears.

"Oh, did he? But why did Rustom take it from you?"

"He had asked me for it many times earlier, and I never parted from it so he snatched it away from me."

"But why did you not give it to him earlier when he asked you for it, Khuda?"

"Why should I? It is mine".

"I have seen Rustom, he does not have any toys for himself, may be his parents could not buy for him, so he looks to you as a friend and expects you to share your toys with him."

"Yes, but what is mine, is mine, he cannot take it away from me like this."

"Yes, I understand, but nothing that we have in this world is ours, everything is given to us by God, so we must learn to share it with others," she said.

"Where is god?" I had questioned this to Zeba many times in the past and she had always explained to me instantaneously.

"When someone is kind to you, when someone loves you, when someone creates a rhythm in your life, that someone is sent by God." It all sounded so bizarre to me, she never forced me to understand anything, and she had her own ways of explaining to me about the most abstract things.

"God smiles at you from heaven when you share your things with others," she continued. "Have I ever told you the story of a poor boy in the town of Isfahan?" she asked me.

Before I could ask her where heaven was, she started narrating the story. "Once upon a time there lived a poor boy in a town. He loved cakes and always dreamt of eating them. That year, there was a famine in his town. One day, a Jinni appeared in front of him and gave him a bag full of cakes and told him that those cakes were different and that he should give them only to those people who had been starving and

Benazir Patil

not eaten for long. The boy felt somewhat annoyed with this; he had been craving for cakes for so long and so he wanted to eat the first piece himself. Just as he was about to, a frail old man came to him and asked for the cake, saying he had not eaten anything for last seven days. The boy felt that he himself had not eaten anything since morning, but he remembered his father teaching him to 'always help the old and share your things with them,' so he gave away that piece of cake to the old man. The boy wandered around a bit and sat under a tree and put his hand for another piece of cake for himself. Just then he saw a cow and two calves dying of hunger with tears falling from their eyes. He had always loved animals and so he fed the cow and the calves with a few pieces. As the boy walked a little ahead, he felt a little unhappy, because as he put his hand in the bag he found that he was left with only two pieces of cake. He decided that he will eat one and take the other for his mother. As he took out one piece for himself, he saw his dear friend rushing to him; he told the boy that because of famine, they had not been able to cook anything for the last three days and since yesterday his mother had taken ill. He asked the boy if he could share the piece of cake with his mother. The boy could not turn down his friend's request and fed his friend's mother with the remaining two pieces. The friend's mother hugged the boy, blessed him, and then he left from there."

"The boy was dejected and continued to walk around with a crestfallen face. The Jinni appeared again and blessed the boy and said, 'God is very happy with you and feels that you are truly generous; he has decided to make you a great man when you grow up.' Saying so, the Jinni went away."

"Years later, when the boy grew up he became the richest farmer of the town who was known for his generosity towards the poor and needy."

I continued listening to her . . .

"You don't need to hide away your treasures for yourselves, you must share them, the joy of sharing is much more than the joy of possessing," said Zeba.

Then onwards, she often told me the stories of Hatem Tai and how he had inherited a sense of generosity from his mother Gonayya. The stories of Hatem and his seven questions, his search for obtaining answers got me so involved that I imagined myself as him, wandering far and wide in search of answers. The most fascinating of all those seven answers was, 'he who speaks the truth is always tranquil'.

3

Oldies of my town, especially those with one foot in the grave, followed this ancient legacy of prophesying when a child was to be born in some house, regardless of what relations they had with that family. They believed that souls that fell down from above followed the same gods in their earthly life as they did in heaven. This meant that the position of the planets at a child's birth would determine the qualities of the soul that settled in the child's body, which also preordained and influenced his or her fate, most importantly, where the Sun was at the moment of birth. One such prophecy must have been due at the time of my birth too, but having not known or heard of it was again a fortune for me rather than an ill-luck as everybody around me considered it to be.

May be the very first humans who gazed at the stars questioned their own loneliness and wondered at the unbelievable vastness of the cosmos, and tried to find some refuge in making measurements of the movements of the heavenly spheres they witnessed. For them, it was difficult to stop there and relating these measurements to a pantheon of gods or the fate of the kings had become both a pleasure and necessity. Uneasiness of the human minds to know more about what their future had in store for them had led the world to many more calculations than just the one I knew of. I do not know if I was a run-of-the-mill case whose disinterestedness in future was common enough or I was exceptional in that sense. I need say nothing here, because nothing can show better than my journey in life whether that prediction about me turned out to be true or false.

Born in the city of seven walls, I had grown listening to the story of seven creations of god; sky was the first part of the world that was created, then water, then earth, then sun, then plants and animals, human beings were the sixth creation, and fire, the seventh and the last one. I was also asked to believe that the world was divided into seven regions or *karshvars* surrounded by the world ocean called *Vorukasha*.

Zeba completely doted on me. Both of us shared a very serene bond, as lucid and pure as the water trickling down from the springs. Comprehending her nature was not that easy; she was different from most women of her times. Pleasant and polite, wise and witty, well-read and well-bred was an apt description of hers. She had perused a thousand books and legends and she could talk endlessly about the bygone men and matters. A heart shaped faced Zeba sometimes came across as clumsy too.

With a much clearer view of the world, her heart had learnt to repel the most material aspects of it and had enabled her to develop mental abilities that made her completely human. As a child she had lived in Khorasan, where her father had been a rich landowner. A war like situation in their hometown had created a tumult enough for them to move out from there and reach Hamadan. The loss of wealth however had led to misery and difficulties so unsurpassable that her parents succumbed to it and grievingly left the world.

The loss of parents had carved out a distinct sense of independence in Zeba and all the situations in her life had mentored her to move towards a not-so-welcome state of renunciation for a woman of such a young age. She had perhaps become a knower who was watchful of everything that was distracting her from God. She had witnessed a life from riches and wealth to sheer dearth. A glimpse of reality that material possessions could be so momentary had made her drift onto this path. Renunciation for her meant that her hands were free of possessing and the heart was free of craving. In the eyes of the world, Zeba stood as a self-righteous human being who believed in relying on God in all its conditions and let Him choose everything for her with an acceptance that God knows best for His children. She was looked upon by many elders who were at a stage of life where repentance on past acts was a routine; they particularly admired Zeba for being much ahead of her times.

In one such moment of contemplation she had come face to face with a different stage of her life, and that was I. She had spent seven years of her life between the death of her parents and my arrival. She considered my presence to be a fortune; she had not only accepted this new direction her life had turned into happily, but had become a vehicle of my happiness. The initial years after her parents left were filled with struggle, a struggle to make both ends meet, to find security and protection, and to lead a lonely life. She had begun to realize that every happening in her life was making her stronger. All that was happening around her was looked at by the world as most calamitous, but for Zeba it was God's will. At a tender age she could conclude that each and every situation in her life was not only giving her a chance to understand the ways of the almighty but was also getting to examine her. A realization that one should never give way to feelings of despair and drudgery was prominent in her mind. That had led her to understand that there is always a reason for what happens to us and what becomes of us in this bestowed life. For Zeba, the concepts of adversity and prosperity were far beyond the way people perceived them. Remembrance of the divine meant prosperity for her and forgetting Him was adversity.

Her brightest smile emerged when people addressed me by the first half of my name. It was Zeba who had given me this name—the reasons were not known to many. Seldom are people interested in knowing the explanations behind how they derived their names; I always was.

⎯⎯◈⎯⎯

The serene sound of *azaan* woke her up to a new world each day; it had an enchanting effect on her mind, it reminded her of the new bounties that lay in store for her.

On one such morning, she had heard a hue and cry outside a house in the neighborhood. A young widow lay dead in the midst of misery. People had eagerly circled around her house and were keen to know about the infant in the lap of an old lady. The widow had been living there for a few years now; she had lost her husband a few months ago. Then onwards, everyone had seen her working as a maid in the nearby palatial mansions. But the arrival of her baby had made things worse for her, she had taken ill and no one got to know about it.

As Zeba approached the crowd, she understood that the commotion had nothing to do with the death of the woman; the concern was about the lonesome child and what would they do with it. Zeba walked up to the old lady holding the child and gazed at the face of the seven-day-old baby, which was as radiant as a sparkling sun, unaware of its situation. She held the baby in her arms and floated in complete tranquility; she felt the touch of those tiny hands; it seemed like a call from divinity, much like the *azaan* she heard every morning. As she stood caressing the child amongst the noisy crowd, the sounds gradually subsided and people watched her with an unusual perception. They knew of her as a savior who provided comfort to those in pain and misery. A

Benazir Patil

contemplation of Zeba's role in the life of the child was not as difficult for them, but they had their own distinctions of judging her: comforting people in pain was one thing and looking after someone for a lifetime was another.

"Are you able to think of a place where we can take this child?" the old lady questioned Zeba with a kinder look.

"Yes!"

"Do you know of some orphanage?" she asked.

"No, not to an orphanage, my home," Zeba responded.

Not many felt startled about this and many even continued to talk amongst themselves, until one old man stepped forward and placed his hand on Zeba's head.

"My child, it is not very easy to take care of someone else's child; today you are alone, tomorrow you may have your husband and then your own children. Let us look for some place where we can take the child," he said.

"I understand, life is like a river which the almighty fills with whatever we deserve; He fills moments of cheer and moments of distractions; today is the moment of cheer because He has bestowed His love on me by telling me that both the child and I deserve each other," Zeba said.

"You are very large-hearted, may you transmit all your holiness to this child and may he grow a divine soul who would convey and share the stories of your selfless acts with the world and spread your religion, which is unique and still unknown to many of us!" the old man blessed her.

Perplexed at the blessing that was bestowed on her, Zeba continued to caress the child as her eyes filled with tears of happiness. It was a strange moment in her life, loaded with a distinctive sense of responsibility and fulfillment at the same time.

That day she named this child that is me, as 'Khudabakhsh', meaning 'gift of god'. The entry of this new entity in her life was to guide her through the purpose for what she had come to this world.

Rumi's words truly befitted her:

"The sign on the road is for travelers who easily become lost. Those who have attained union with God, have no need for signs or roads, they have the inward eye and divine lamp."

Has the world witnessed it more often that when one brings up someone else's child, one becomes more devoted, possibly because those are not the ties of possession and claims but merely of affection? I had become an apple of her eye. A *dervish* in Zeba had got converted to a loving mother. She was now busy raising me and recreating a munificent human out of me. I also could never conceive any two thoughts about anything and looked upon her for every little thing I needed.

Selfless Love! The quest continued in the minds of people who saw us together. There lay a lot of questions in their minds, but none in hers.

Moulded by her own thoughts, she was guided by the feelings of selflessness that gave her joy in everything she did. No words could reveal the secret of her happiness as she glided into this new companionship. What others thought of me was a complete contrast from what I thought of myself. My unhappy loss or want of something was a given discussion for everyone around, an illusion of my unfulfilled dreams, life led under an umbrella of sympathy. Referring me as an orphan at times did appear to be brutal as against the reality that was the truth of me being the most loved child on earth.

Zeba alone was definitely incapable of re-affirming this fact to mankind. Nevertheless, the fact that her life was not devoid of defeats and transformations was of no consequence to her.

"*Behešt zīr pāy-e mādarān ast*"(paradise lies at mothers' feet), was the very first truth I had met with.

4

"You love watching these stars, don't you?" Zeba asked, watching me keenly looking at the sky, dark but filled with strangely sparkling luminous bodies.

"I wonder about them, are they very far from us?" I asked her.

"Indeed, they are far, but we can still see them. There are millions of them around the earth, but not all can be seen," she said.

"Do you know all these stars?" I asked.

"I have read about many of them, but there are these seven which are known to us from ancient times, the ones that can cast their magical spell on us."

"Magical spell?"

"Yes, these seven visible planets were the first Gods of the ancient man," she said.

"Which seven planets?"

"The sun, the moon and the five planets that move around the Earth—Saturn, Jupiter, Mars, Venus and Mercury" said Zeba pointing fingers at the sparkling bright Venus.

"But why were they considered Gods?"

"Humanity believed that their survival depended on these seven. They alone ruled the entire universe, every change in their lives was caused due to the moods of these planets and they were the tellers of the past, the present and the future," she said.

"What does that mean?"

"It means that the planets conspired together to cause good and bad to us, their movements in the space made a difference to our lives, each of them sent us some energy that acted on us. Interestingly, we got the names of our days from these seven heavenly bodies that we kept on watching for long".

"What energies?"

"These spiritual energies"

"So the gods actually stay there and send us their energies?" I asked her again

"May be," she responded with a big smile and continued:

"The ancient man considered the Sun as the soul of the universe, the life force that sustains everything on Mother Earth. Its rays drive every breath, feeling, belief, inspiration and deed, the strength of its rays helps us transform, and it is the only light in our life, so it was no different from God."

"And the moon?"

"The moon gave us peace and warmth at night so we started worshipping it."

"Oh, I looked at the sun and the moon as my elder brothers, one who walked with me during the day and the other who reflected a special light for me at night," I said.

"It is natural for us to develop that bond, Khuda; we think of them as our companions, they accompany us on our spiritual journey. Jupiter, the giant became the God of sky and thunder, the lord of power manifested his influence by punishing the liars and the unjust," she said.

"Which are the other four?"

"Mars, the red ball, became the God of war. Some people also believe that he is the son of Earth," she said.

"And what about the wonderful Venus?"

"Venus is the only one considered as the Goddess—'the Goddess of love'. The forest dwellers still gaze at her and communicate with their loved ones who have departed from this world. The other is Mercury; it stays closest to the Sun and is the God of Intelligence."

"And the seventh one?"

"Saturn, with its famous rings, is the god of abundance, one who carries a sickle in his hand, some people consider him the deliverer of Justice," she responded and continued:

"These seven sacred lords rule the seven days of our week."

"Oh, perhaps the seven rays of rainbow are also sent by them, isn't it?" I questioned her.

"May be!" she again smiled and added:

"These seven lords have seven colours to themselves, but of all the colours, white is the colour of the Sun. It seemingly is the absence of all colours, yet in reality it is the perfect unity of all the colours. It is akin to the almighty; it contains all colours but is contained in no colour and so symbolizes freedom from all states of consciousness, leading to a spirit of purity and resurgence. And so the day of the sun is the day of resurrection," she said.

"White, it is also the colour of your clothes, I have never seen you wearing any other colour on you, Zeba?" I questioned her again.

"The first day is the day of the Moon, it is a day meant for the departed souls, the souls who yearn for salvation; the second day is the day of Mars, it is the day of evolution; the third day is the day of Mercury and is the day of healing: the fourth day is the day of Jupiter, it is the day of generosity; the fifth is that of Venus, the day of spiritual love; the sixth day belongs to Saturn, Saturn is considered to be the planet of death, but death means a gate to new life, it means a completion of one cycle and starting of a new one, and so an ending of one life clearly means beginning of another one. This is why the sixth day belongs to Saturn and the seventh belongs to Sun, because only after the death can resurrection happen," she said without responding to my earlier question.

"And so all of these days and the planets are associated with different colours?" I asked.

"Yes, they are, now let us sleep, I will tell you a story about it tomorrow," she caressed my head and put me off to bed humming a melody.

I had developed a godly attachment with her. Unlike most of my friends, I had inherited a fortune of bliss and enlightenment sans all the material possessions that they were happy with, which nonetheless had not deterred me from being possessive of my most priceless belonging: Zeba, my very own mother.

5

Taher insisted that I go with him to his village with his father, Saroush.

Saroush was a fantastic potter and my love for pottery had made me spend hours at their place. Together, Taher and I would study after receiving scolding.

"Khuda, be very careful when you are travelling tomorrow, learn to take care of yourself," Zeba said while I was busy preparing for the travel. She seemed worried. I was to be away from her for the first time since I was born.

The next morning, with immense excitement, I walked out of my small hutment to join some strangers along with Taher and his father. We were travelling to Susa. Six of us with four horses. Taher and I mounted on the horses, accompanying the elders on theirs. Following the route mapped by the caravans, we travelled consecutively for two days and reached Susa.

As we entered the town, my eyes twinkled at the site of a beautiful mosque. Saroush asked us to stop there, freshen up and pray. Taher and I showed no interest in praying and disappeared quietly to explore the mosque. Near one of the minarets, we met a handsome young man; he smiled at us, as if he knew us always. He came to us and caressed my head. Though startled at his behaviour, I instantly felt at peace, and all my objections to his presence departed.

"I am Daniyaal," said he.

"But I don't know you," I said, perceiving my blunder at the very next moment.

"You can consider me your friend, now that you have met me."

"I can call you my friend only after Zeba confirms that I can befriend you," I said innocently.

"Sure, I can come with you and meet Zeba," he responded, without enquiring who she was.

His instant proposal to come and meet her sounded weird. But I continued talking to him out of some strange excitement. Strangely, a queer feeling inside was bringing jitters to the stomach. Zeba always talked about young men who conversed sweetly to small children, gave them sweets, kidnapped them and took them to far off land and sold them as slaves. My mind, however, kept on saying that Daniyaal was different; he looked divine, just like an angel.

Since childhood, I had had this strange habit of making friends for no reasons. I wondered if I ever made an effort to find a friend or friendships just happened to me. I never had to start any conversations. I was fortunate to meet people who understood my silence more than my words. Each one who entered my life had a reason to be there. Some entered for a short time and left, some were there to teach, some to seek learning, some to help me sail through my difficulties, and some to seek help for themselves. But each of them was god-sent. There were some who were there to meet and part and then meet again, because they were meant for a lifetime.

Daniyaal introduced himself to Saroush, as the care-taker of the mosque; he offered to take Taher and me around the town to see places. Saroush accepted the deal with little hesitation, and cared more for our excitement, which was profusely visible on our faces.

In the evening as the two of us went and sat with Daniyaal on the pavement near the well, he put his hand in the pocket of his embroidered cloak and brought out some *ajil-e-shirin* for us. Tremendously delicious, we finished all of it. In some time, my eyes felt heavy and I fell asleep. I put my head in his lap and slept. I woke up after an hour's time.

I gazed at Daniyaal and asked "where do you want to take me?"

"To some shrines here, you have been there before," he said.

"I do not remember if I have been there, but how do you know that I have been there?" I asked.

Daniyaal ignored my question and continued, "Khuda, were you dreaming of something?"

I almost jumped and said, "Yes, I was."

"So tell me what you saw in your dream."

Just as I was about to explain the dream, I realized that I had forgotten everything and could not recall one bit. I had often remembered and told my dreams to Zeba, but that moment I had suddenly got busy thinking about Daniyaal, our travel and the places where he was to take us along.

"Why did you want to know about my dream?" I asked him.

"Because I can tell you more about it."

"How do you do that?"

"I can just tell you what your dream means if you tell me what you dreamt."

"Are dreams of any consequence, I see them and often forget what I had seen."

"The dream is certain, and the interpretation thereof sure," Daniyaal proclaimed as if he were a king. He then looked at me, lowered his voice and started explaining: "the dreams are an act of God, they are definite acts. God has His own ways of sharing His will and wish on how we lead our lives. Dream is one of them."

What Daniyaal mentioned about dreams sounded very exciting. I cursed myself for forgetting all that I had dreamt.

"How do I recall my dream Daniyaal?" I said with little frustration. Taher was listening to our conversation with much excitement.

"Next time when you get up from your sleep, just close your eyes and recall what you have dreamt and tell me," he said offering some more delicious *ajil-e-shirin* to both of us.

"This has date, pistachios, hazelnuts, almonds, chickpeas, raisins, and mulberries, seven things mixed together to bless you with divine energy, this will help you remember some of your dreams," he said as we continued to relish the sweets.

"But how do you know that God talks to us in our dreams," Taher interrupted, after much patience.

"Dreams are just one of His ways, we can even listen to His talks in many different ways," said Daniyaal

Both Taher and I were drawn into the excitement of what he was explaining to us.

"Look here," he said, touching his palm on my forehead. "Can you feel something?"

"Yes."

"What can you feel?"

"Something strange, as if, er . . . . , some sound, something . . . as if you are pouring something into my head."

"Right here is your third eye; it attracts vibrations as a magnet does. If you are attentive, there is a lot you can understand."

"Like?"

"Like the good and the bad, fruitions and catastrophes, the laughter and the tears."

"From where?"

"From everything that is around you."

"How?"

"Like this, come let's bend down," he instructed us to prostrate on the ground.

"Touch your forehead to the ground. Quietly, your third eye will absorb the waves."

"What waves?" I reacted without lifting my head.

"Quiet! Listen to the Mother Earth."

Taher and I wondered about everything Daniyaal was telling us, but now we were keen to absorb the waves and listen to the Mother Earth.

I could hear something distinctly, wondered if there was some whispering that the earth was doing to the trees or to me, it was a strange language, I had not learned it yet.

"Can you hear the Mother Earth?" he asked us.

"Yes, some strange sounds," replied Taher and they both continued to converse.

I could vaguely hear their conversation, as if it was occurring in some faraway land. I was completely lost in the vibrations that were reaching me. For a moment, the sound was like anger, I felt as if something around was trying to uproot me but some force beneath was holding me to stay there.

"Now you may raise your head Khuda and sit up," Daniyaal caressed my head and asked me to get up. Taher was up much earlier when he had called for us and I had not responded at all.

I sat up, with a strange sense of freshness; my eyes sparkled. He looked at me and said, "The energy from the earth has reinvigorated you, it has added some lustre to your being, and the rest is the effect of your own blood."

Nonplussed, I struggled to understand his explanations, I had heard from Zeba about the celestial energies coming to us from the seven sacred planets. Was Daniyaal also referring to something similar?

"We have been given the power to understand everything that happens around us, but the loss of attentiveness has caused a lot of loss to humankind, just as the sun guides us with light, Mother Earth guides us through her energies; these influence our thoughts, decisions and actions."

"How?"

"Touching Mother Earth has activated your third eye; this has refreshed your attentiveness and receptivity. Slowly, you will learn to listen to her, you will understand how to absorb the energies she radiates and one day you will realize that your entire being is being nourished with her affection for you," he said.

"What do you understand when you listen to her?" I asked.

"Sometimes I understand that she is happy when she transfers all her best energies to me, sometimes I can hear her cry, sometimes I can feel her reacting to the degradation of human mind, sometimes she advises me and sometimes, she helps me in forgiving people," he said.

"And why does she do that?"

"Here, this surface you are standing on is the outermost layer of her soul, she possesses a soul of immeasurable depth, and it is sevenfold. You and I are incapable of seeing the other six layers. But, when we talk to her she tells us all that lies in her hidden soul," he said.

"What lies in her hidden soul?"

"All that we say, we do and we contemplate."

"What does she do with that?"

"Because she is our mother, she absorbs all the good and the bad that we do, say and think so as to remind us of our apathy when we turn ruthless and our joy when we turn virtuous."

The act of listening to Mother Earth was definitely new, but prostration was not. What Daniyaal shared resonated with what Zeba frequently mentioned: "Prostration in prayers would guide us to an understanding of '*Al-Bayyinat*', a state of perfect visions."

My sheer eagerness compelled me to spell this out to Daniyaal.

"Yes. She is right, you prostrate twice not without a purpose. In the first you declare, 'from this earth, you have created me and have taken me out' and in the second, you accept 'to this earth you will return me and take me out again'. You realize that you have been born of this earth and you will go back to her," he said.

"How fascinating!" I exclaimed to myself.

Absolutely speechless, we sat, trying to grasp all that Daniyaal had revealed.

6

I had been playing with my friends since afternoon. As I entered the house, Zeba asked me to do the ablutions in preparation for the evening prayers.

"Do not forget to wash your eyes. Every sin you thought of committing will come out of your eyes and flow out with the water. Do not forget to wash your feet, every sin towards which your feet walked will come off with the water, the holy Prophet instructed us!" Zeba exclaimed every time I made a fuss over doing the ablutions.

Nevertheless, the stories of *Ab-e-Hayaat* and *Ab-e-Zamzam* were a part and parcel of our story bag that opened while she put me to bed every night.

An incredible blend of modesty and willpower, I had always known Zeba as my mother. Several souls in Lalejin invited me with witnesses to share the realities of my birth; I often overheard that my father died a few months before my birth and my mother succumbed to a treacherous epidemic when I was just seven days old. But Zeba had filled the memories of my early years with utter joy and happiness. Once when I shared a serious concern about not having any sibling, she had sweetly responded she did not want to give away all the love she had stored for me to anybody else and so the siblings were never called for.

After dinner, I asked her: "Zeba, have we been to Susa before?"

"Yes," she said a little hesitatingly.

"When?"

"Long time ago, but how do you know? You were too young to remember anything."

"No, I do not remember anything. I met Daniyaal, the caretaker of the mosque there, and he told me that I had been to Susa as a child."

"Who Daniyaal?" she asked me furiously. I could gauge her anger over my mingling with strangers.

"He is a friend; I met him when I went to Susa with Taher. A strange but wonderful person, he talks about Mother Earth and the language she speaks to her children. Like you, he is a bundle of tales and anecdotes. He also told us about different rivers of the world, the forests in Africa, the deserts in Sahara; he can even be a Hakim for the unwell. But he has one unusual way of expression," I said.

"What is that?" she asked.

"He repeats phrases and declares them like a king does; when I questioned him about their meaning, he said that I should just remember the words and not worry about their meaning, because the understanding will reach me when it is supposed to."

"What phrases does he repeat?"

"He often says—'I give wisdom unto the wise and knowledge to them that know understanding.'"

There appeared a changed expression on Zeba's face that I could not comprehend. Her intuitive mind reflected something; a long chain of thoughts ran through her mind, as if she knew what those words really meant and who Daniyaal was.

"What are you thinking, Zeba?" I asked.

She looked at me with an intense sense of insecurity. She was not the kind who would get overwhelmed by anything, I had yet to see someone as calm as her. Her introspective mind signaled her about her attachment with me. When in all these years Zeba had become virtually detached to everything around her, what was the attachment with me all about? For the first time her longing for my nearness to her had surfaced on her mind.

Every time I talked about the distinctiveness of Daniyaal, it triggered Zeba's thoughts to know more. I was yet to tell her about how Daniyaal had taught me to listen to Mother Earth.

"Do you know that earth is our mother?" I asked her.

"Earth is everything to us, we all come from her and we go back to her, and we are a part of her," she said.

"But you said we go back to God and have come from Him?" I questioned.

"It is God who has blessed us with Mother Earth. She produces us and produces all that we need for our living, tirelessly, all from herself!"

"Sometimes I wonder about God. Does He really exist? Has anybody seen Him? Have you ever doubted His existence?" I asked with an expression as if I was committing a great sin by doing that.

"Why do you dread asking me something like this, Khuda?" She at once gauged my state of mind.

"Prophet Abraham too once asked this question to God. He wanted to know how God could instil life into a dead person. God then demonstrated the miracle to him. So all of us get these doubts in our mind and it is best to seek the answer from God himself. He has His own ways of demonstrating His presence," she said.

7

In the Madrasa, I often heard the stories of *Isa* and *Musa* along with those of Mohammad, Ibrahim and Jibraeel from the Imam who ardently taught me the verses. The stories of *Isa* impressed me the most. But I remained confused; sometimes I got to hear about his resurrection, sometimes about him being called back by Allah, dwelling in the fourth layer of heaven.

That day, after returning from the Madrasa, my senses were as usual set on my most beloved character of the angelic stories. I went to Zeba and quietly asked her "Was *Isa* a Muslim?"

"There was no Islam when *Isa* was born; he was the founder of Christianity," responded Zeba with a smile.

"If *Isa* was not a Muslim, then how is it that he was called back by Allah, how is it that he is still alive and lives in the fourth heaven with him?" I passionately re-questioned her.

She immediately grasped that it was not worth responding to her gifted son in such a matter-of-fact manner. The strangeness in my idiosyncrasies at times worried her but day after day, my questions were giving her more clarity about how I perceived the world around me. What also worried her were my interactions with the *dervishes* clad in black robes carrying an oval pot along with a chain of weird but attractive beads. It was indeed startling, despite being a *dervish* herself who had renounced almost everything, she was uncomfortable about my mingling with other *dervishes*.

Attuned to wearing a *Rusari* (veil) around her head that swung onto her body; she was much adorned by natural jewels: the smile she wore was no less than glittering pearls; her twinkling eyes felt like sparkling stars in the sky. For me, Zeba was the queen Sheherzaad who told me stories of valor and magic before I fell asleep. Her soul rejuvenated when she told me stories of '*Uru-Salim*', the holy city of three religions.

"A place where the Jews built their first temple," she would start.

"Is a place where *Isa* was crucified, it stood as the first *qiblah* for the Muslims even before they turned towards *Kaabah*," she said.

"But is not Rome also a city of pilgrimage?" I asked.

"Indeed, different people go to different places for pilgrimage. Apart from being revered by pilgrims as holy, they have one strange similarity."

"What is that?"

"All three are built on seven hills. People who revere these should be living like brothers but the sheer survival of this brotherhood has been an endless struggle."

Zeba often imagined all of them praying together; many times I caught her imagination and flattered her subtly.

"Are you that priestess, Zeba? Guiding them to pray together?"

"Yes, that is how God would have wanted of us, but we have divided ourselves in countless sects. We have forgotten His purpose of bringing us into this world," she casually responded. Her inclination and interest in discussing factual

Benazir Patil

and conceptual complexities of the religion that we both were living with was enormous.

"The world has experienced evolution in the true sense, Khuda. It has seen the fall of empires and the rise of Messiahs who guided and died for the good and the bad of their fellow-beings, by being eternal, extending forgiveness, and toiling for salvation to all who believed in them," she said.

A contemplation that the world was still following the course of receiving Messiahs that brought messages from the spirit, and that it was the spirit that engraved our destinies, was always prime on her mind.

"Humans are not very different from all the other animals that God has created," she explained to me with a firm belief. "One aspect that makes us distinct from others is our concern for ourselves before our concern for Mother Nature, our self-centredness. Animals, however, dwell in harmony with nature; their pursuit of a prey is linked to their hunger, not to their intention to accumulate. Humans exploit every element of this universe to fulfil their desires."

My mind could not conceive what the term 'universe' meant every time she referred to it.

"What do you mean by 'universe', Zeba?"

"The holy books say that God created this universe, this whole space that we use and consider our possession rightfully; He took seven days to do that. On the first day, He created light and defined the day and night for us; on the second day He created waters and He told us what was above the land, the sky and what lay below the land, the water; on the third day He created plants to give us food from them; on the fourth day He created the sun, moon and stars to rule the day and night; and then on the fifth day He created fish to fill the waters and birds to fill the sky."

"It looks like God worked very hard in creating this universe; was He doing it all alone, Zeba"

"Yes, Khuda, on the sixth day He created man and animals and gave plants as food to them, and after doing this He was so tired that He gave himself rest on the seventh day."

I was immensely delighted to hear the story of creation. I almost thought of walking to His house to hear more about all the troubles He faced while doing this mammoth task.

The Principles of Truth are Seven; he who knows these, understandingly, possesses the Magic Key before whose touch all the Doors of the Temple fly open

The Kybalion

8

Living in the town of Hamadan, I often came face to face with antiquity. Over and over again my village friends from Lalejin who made excellent ceramic pots impressed me. I often told Zeba that one-day I will learn to make these beautiful pots.

Mischievously she would question me "For whom?"

And smilingly I would respond, "Rubina".

"It was the Assyrians first, then the Mongols, and finally the Ottomans who attacked Hamadan, but the city stood against each courageously," said Rubina. A storehouse of magnificent tales, she often came and stayed with us. I played with her endlessly in the open space in front of our house, and then when we both got tired, we would go inside and hover around Zeba when she had busied herself with cooking. After we finished with dinner, I put my head in her lap and listened to the stories of wars and grandeur.

"Why so many attacks?" I asked.

"The mighty kings and their armies put in all their force and struggled to grab more and more land for their empire."

The stories of the kings and queens that ruled in and around Hamadan took me to the world of weapons and wars beyond the borders of Persia. Almost a sister to Zeba, she spoke of historical lineages of these dynasties as though she had lived with them for years. A completely different worldview entered my imagination as I heard of wars that were fought between the belligerent kings.

The altered acts of inhumanity that arose since the inception of the world were nothing but stories of increasing needs of men. How awfully true it is that no culture could ever be an exception to these unfortunate incidents called wars. Influenced by religion, culture or personal greed, they occurred nevertheless in every nook and corner of the world. The epics and masterpieces too glorified the return of the victorious heroes from war, with trivial explanation of bloodshed. Tales of grandeur and nobility, independence and sacrifice enhanced the attraction for war, mobilized men, and reflected myriad romantic ideas of what the wars intended.

Keener to know more about the nature and attitudes of individual kings rather than how they ruled, I questioned Rubina on their behaviour.

"Tell me who these kings were; were they like you and me or different from us?"

Rubina made tireless efforts to tell me about the benevolence and cruelties that kings dwelled in with their subjects. She was slowly beginning to grasp that I often pondered why people behaved the way they did. It was novel to her when I explained the attributes that perhaps guided these rulers.

"Khuda, the common people suffered when their reigns ended. Sometimes people had to move from one kingdom to another because a change of the king meant change of religion and ideology. It started racial conflicts among them, and they got carried away by the religion the king followed. There would be no choice left but to leave their belongings and migrate to evade persecution that resulted from ethnic wars."

"So strange! People should revolt against such kings," I said.

"When the earth was created, all lived together, with no one being a king and no one a subject, since nobody wanted any power over the other. There were no wars, but as man started possessing things and realized the importance of possessions, gradually his ego was born and this put him through the test of competition where he learned to win over others and started displaying his powers. This whole process continued by leaps and bounds and resulted in chaos, a state of war which only led to some of them winning and some of them losing. Wars were fought for riches, principles, rights and many more things, but soon the cause of war became secondary to war itself, and we moved into an age where nothing could be settled without anything lesser than blood-shed of innocents," Rubina said.

"Why do innocents have to die?" I asked.

"Because it is they who have to fight for the kings; it is they who make the armies for us to protect us."

"Is not this ridiculous? One ruler rules and others have to follow the ruler and the rules? Why can we not live without all this, Rubina?" I asked.

"Yes, we can, but we humans need to be governed by some things, some rules and some laws, otherwise it will be difficult to live peacefully. It is these rulers who created the laws of the land, to govern us uniformly. But sadly, these laws distinguished us from each other and created disparities. Whenever these disparities rise to a level of intolerance, people revolt against the rulers," she intently explained to me.

I could comprehend the phases in the life of civilizations when people felt the need to revolt against the mounting tyrannies. The revolutions were neither stories nor events, but sagas enunciated with immense pride. From time to time, a need for a fresh commencement of society with better decrees did become seeming, but to get that rolling, people kept paying an incredibly colossal price.

Glorifying the concept of 'might is right' was something philosophers also loved. Man has been crossing one era after another filled with a hysterical rush towards fortune, impulses to rise, expand and lead. The undying plans of expansion are always married to the assumption of assuring prosperity to the common people. Despite living in peace and calmness, many people around gave me enough understanding of the chaos emerging from the struggle for land that always replaced the tranquillity brought about by the prophets. Wars of a deeper nature and greater perpetuity were as much a part of human lives.

As much the stories of kings interested me, hearing of the woes caused by wars disturbed my mind.

✦

One night I lay thinking in my bed about all that I had heard from Rubina. I got up and walked to Zeba as she continued to weave a quilt for us under the faint light. Without getting distracted by the thought of brightness she needed for putting the stitches, I told her: "I read one more story of *Isa* today." She gave me a strange look, because she often wondered how I managed to read the less available stories of *Isa* in the land we lived.

"What did you read?"

"Once, when a mob came to arrest *Isa*, one of His followers tried to defend Him with a sword. But *Isa* asked Him to put his sword back into its place saying 'for all those who take up the sword shall perish by the sword'; later many of

Isa's followers were martyred for their faith, but never used violence to resist their fate." I said.

"I know, the world may continue with sins of all kinds, but those who truly belong to the kingdom of God are called to put their total trust in him and to obey *Isa's* teachings against violence," she said.

Zeba knew that the stories I heard from Rubina were teaching me the culture around, one that was splitting every moment into antagonistic factions, encouraging people to subdivide themselves into the smallest of groups waging ruthless wars against each other. But, she was hopeful that the clamours in society also called for a transformed reality that would assure peace to all.

While Zeba gave me a real depiction of what I should be like, Rubina gave me a palpable image of what society was like. Sometimes the thoughts expressed by both of them confused me so badly that I suspected if I was a misfit in this civilization.

My heart, however, told me a different tale. It was telling me a story of my emergence from the 'myself of childhood' to the 'myself of youth' and progressing to 'my genuine mature self'. It said that I had to wait and find out the changes that would occur in the way I thought, interpreted and reacted. Layers of experiences were struggling to heap layers and layers of character onto me. What I was to become was not known to me. I was no unfortunate exception, rarely is it known to anyone.

9

"Jamshid," Ferdowsi wrote, "was the king who built the city of Ecbatana". The city supposedly had seven walls, each having a different color, with the inner wall made out of gold. Considered to be a ruler of the world by his people; his subjects feared him for all the powers he possessed; they believed that he controlled the angels and the demons. As he looked into his seven-ringed magical cup, he fell into a trance and visualized the deep truths and realities of the world. He could hear voices and see images in it; slowly he could visualize the future. Whatever the cup revealed became his vision, he acknowledged this as a divine blessing and did all the good he could for his kingdom. Prosperity spread her arms and touched all, so much so that no one lived in poverty. His divinity soon left him with a sense of grandeur and he started playing with it. The revelations from the cup made him influential enough to reason like a creator, the pride reached its zenith, causing his subjects to kill him one day.

Every child in Hamadan had heard the story of Jamshid. Every time I heard it, what struck me most were the seven rings of his cup and the seven walls he built around the city. A sense of curiosity arose in my mind, and I could think of none other than Daniyaal who I could ask what it really meant. My inquisitiveness compelled me to open the *Ketaab-e-Hayaat* to look for knowledge on Jamshid and his miraculous cup. I opened it on a page randomly as Daniyaal had suggested and found the page completely blank. At once, I recalled the seven occasions Daniyaal had mentioned; curiosity was not one of them. I realized my mistake and put the book in its place. A revelation that the *Ketaab-e-Hayaat* was no different from the cup of Jamshid occurred to me. I was not to misuse it, if only I did that, I would not obtain the wisdom it bequeathed me. I felt delighted about this new understanding I had received. I closed my eyes and thanked the almighty.

"Why do all the kings have so much pride? Are they different from us?" I asked Zeba.

"No, they are just like any of us, the pride seeps into their minds due to the riches that they possess, and that can happen to us also, why only the kings," she said.

"Why did God make us like this, he should have not let us have this pride"

"God made us in his own image. There is a story of God conversing with *Musa*," she said.

My eyes twinkled and Zeba at once sensed the joy burgeoning inside me.

"Once God said to *Musa* that he made man in His own image, according to His likeness, so that man may rule over the fish of the sea, the birds of the sky, the beasts, over the whole earth and over every creeping thing that creeps on earth.

Then *Musa* requested God, 'I pray you, show me your glory' and God responded, 'I am who I am' and then he revealed to *Musa* his seven divine selves.

So the first thing God revealed about himself is that He is compassionate. Then He told *Musa* the second fact about himself that He is gracious. The third thing He revealed was that He is slow to anger. The fourth fact was that He is abounding in love and kindness and He extends His divine mercies to those in need. The fifth fact was He is abundant in truth and faithfulness; He is reliable. God's Word is as sure as His character. The sixth fact was that He is forgiving and is always willing to forgive. The seventh was 'Not erasing the consequences of sin'. The last phrase in God's self-revelation to *Musa* reflected on the consequences of sin". She said and paused for a moment.

"So my child, it is with these seven divine qualities that He created us."

Was God similar to Man or was Man to be like God? Multitude of questions erupted like volcanoes in my mind. It meant clearly that God created us with His own attributes and wanted us to be like Him, but what Rubina said about the struggling men was not similar to what God revealed to *Musa* about Himself. What Jamshid tried to do also was not what God expected of us, then how were we supposed to be and what were we supposed to do after being born into this world? I felt as if Man was struggling to run away from these attributes. We were created from the dust and went back to the dust is what Daniyaal had mentioned when he made us hear the voice of Mother Earth. We became living only when God had instilled a living soul and life breath in us.

"Why did God make Man in His own image?" I asked her—I could not resist myself! She was a little startled, but there was nothing in this world that she had not answered.

"Do you remember your lesson on '*al-ensān al-kāmel*', where your teacher had once described to you what a complete human being should be like, one who lived in and was guided by the divine light of the lord, one who was a mere

Benazir Patil

reflection of God, one who was born with divine attributes of the creator?" she said.

"Yes, and he also said that we remain incomplete because we get entangled with worldly pleasures and get blinded," I said excitedly.

"Absolutely, my son!" Zeba exclaimed caressing my cheeks.

"The attributes of a complete human being are the attributes of God aptly mirrored in our nature. God has innumerable qualities, to be completely human is being able to imitate these divine qualities in everyday life, and to be like Him is our inherent destiny. We just need to remain conscious, sentient enough to listen to the spirit within".

"Do you know someone with such divine qualities?" I asked her.

"I do not know if the end of the world is soon coming, but it is true that such people continue to be born to sustain the rebirth of this turbulent universe. They are blessed with the rare combination of wisdom of the world and devotion in their eyes." Uttering this she looked at me with wonder and spoke to me in a language I had never heard before.

"Rebirth of the world!" I exclaimed with surprise.

"Yes, the earth gets so badly affected by the merciless acts of men that she finds it difficult to survive and gets rejuvenated every time a blessed soul is born in her arms."

"I do not understand what you say."

"You will, one day. You too have been given a birth to bring about this rebirth, a time will come when the almighty will guide you to experience the language of Mother Earth and assimilate her music in your mind".

I wondered if Zeba was referring to what Daniyaal had taught me. I had refrained from sharing it with her; I wanted to master the art first.

10

The hour had struck; I was not sure what I was reacting to. I had seen people growing old, old enough till they were unable to walk, hear or talk. Though I had never thought of Zeba's old age, at the back of my beyond I was aware that like all the others, one day she would also grow old.

Weeks after weeks had passed; she was deteriorating with every passing day. She was strong and I always wondered if she ever got tired, but the illness just overpowered her in all its completeness, the feebleness on her face was evident.

There was something that severely troubled my mind. It was not about the end of her life, it was about the direction my life was going in. At fourteen, I was turning intuitive about my lonely journey where Zeba would cease to be my caretaker, but that was it; I could understand no more than that.

My mind was battling through the moments of numbness and dejection.

It was a chilly winter evening. Since morning Zeba had complained on and off of feeling terribly cold and I had kept on spreading blankets over her to keep her warm. The local doctor had visited her two days ago and had asked me to be brave and face it. 'Face it' meant what? He had not said a word beyond that. Zeba had not been sleeping enough, but whenever she slept for a little while, I turned to a corner and cried silently. I was oblivious to how the tears kept rolling down my cheeks. Deep inside I was sad about something, as if I was going to lose something very precious in life. It was Zeba who had been teaching me to give up things easily and live life sans attachments, but Zeba was no attachment. She was the light of my life, my only companion who I looked up to in all my predicaments and happiness.

There were people who came home to see her, who 'consoled' me with stories of epidemics: "Families and families just got erased leaving no single member to survive." I was not in a state of mind to think if they were talking sense; I had only one question to myself and to the spirit that I believed in: why should Zeba die? Who would love me and care for me after she is gone? My selfishness of wanting her meant asking her to stay alive and asking God to not let her die. The child inside me found it overwhelming to think of living without her, what was I to do? I had never imagined anything beyond Zeba. I knew I had come to the world to do some good, but I was not prepared to do that good without her.

I had heard that in the land of the *Vedas*, people believed in re-birth, a person would come to life, and die and be reborn; taking seven births was common. Traditions said, a being with impeccable kindness and spirituality shall not have more than one birth, but those who failed to commit good deeds would come back to the world to make up for the sins in their earlier birth. One had to move from the mistakes of earlier life to perfection in the next birth.

I thought deeply if Zeba would be reborn. Her kindness could become an impediment in bringing her back to this world.

"Death is not a great loss, my son, it is just a parting from this body to an unknown world." It was two years ago when she had suddenly started this conversation with me when our neighbor Yusuf had succumbed to death.

"A greater loss is when people live this life like they were dead". She had her own ways of making me aware of the processes we go through from the time of our birth till we die. She perhaps wanted me to know that I should be able to envisage a life after her.

"The temporal nature of life is an inevitable truth. We all grow up to believe that we were born one day, and shall also die one day. What we never want to believe is that one-day could be any day. We all believe in the future, and plan our lives always with a positive feeling that we have come to this world to do many things and that is how we should be living life."

"What happens to us after we die?" I asked her without being wary of why she was explaining about death to me.

"My dear, since the birth of this world, nobody has come back to tell us what happened to them after they died. However, when we look around, we know that in universe there is steadiness in everything and human life cannot be exempted from this movement. Our existence cannot be un-informed and disengaged from the rhythms of this cosmos. Our existence too is a constant, vibrant process of transformation. Just the way the stars, trees, animals are born, live and complete their expected life; we humans too die and persist after death in a form that is not known to us. The vivacious liveliness called life is like a stream, which has neither a beginning nor an end. It just means that we are moving from one form to another," she explained, watching my face full of questions and confusions.

She was trying to explain to me that if she ever dies, she will not be going anywhere away but will continue to live with me in some form or the other—very much near me—but this was difficult to contemplate. Human beings are so attuned to sensing things tangibly.

After a deep slumber of a few hours, Zeba had awakened. She looked at me and understood that a question was in the offing, but she did not pay any heed to that. She herself wanted to say something. But her expressions were different than usual, they conclusively did not display any anguish but ensured certainty of her thoughts.

"But why should you die so early Zeba? You are not old!" I mumbled to myself with utter impatience.

"What are you saying, Khuda?" she asked me as if my words had reached her ears. I was taken aback because I was sure that I was talking to myself and had not said anything loudly to her.

She was the same Zeba who had rescued me, a seven-day-old baby, after my parents' untimely death. Her immense emotionality had only generated immense strength in her and she was trying to bestow all of that onto me.

She had been living a life beyond my comprehension. What I could understand of her, however, was the depth of her soul, her immense honesty, the love she radiated, her full faith in the spirit and the messages she spread through her virtuous living. She was my first teacher who had taught me to look inward and measure my acts.

Her every act was like meditation.

"My parting from you will give you pain, I know that, but all of us have to live life through experiencing both sadness and happiness; none of these emotions can ever remain constant, my child," she said. Her words triggered tears in my eyes. I could not stop myself from speaking my heart out, and I wept like a baby. I was yet to understand what pain I would go through without her presence and the parting was something I was unprepared for.

"Many centuries ago, there lived a great sage in India called Siddhartha; the world gradually started calling him 'the Buddha' meaning 'the enlightened one'. He also lost his mother when he was just seven days old. Just like you are questioning me now, he also asked questioned to himself about his mother's death. This question of life and death made him discard all worldly desires and go in search of truth. A child born in the house of king, had to suffer sorrows too! Though he rolled in luxuries, he could not be kept away from the distress that life had in-store for him. He realized that everything in life was ephemeral and nothing would last."

I could not fathom what Zeba was talking about. What did the Buddha have to do with Zeba's death? However, I listened quietly to what she was saying. She spoke at her own pace.

"One day, while wandering into the forest, a woman came to him with her child, completely grief stricken. She told him that her child lay dead in her arms, and she requested the Buddha to help her in bringing back her child to life. The Buddha saw the dead child and told her that if she is able to get some poppy seeds, he will make a medicine out of the seeds that can help rejuvenate the child's life. As she turned to go and fetch the seeds, he mentioned to her that she should bring the seeds from that home where no death had occurred. The grieving mother went to every household in the village, but she could not find a home where there had been no death ever. Exhausted, she came back to the Buddha, along with the realization that grief and pain of parting of loved ones through death was as much an occurrence as was joy and happiness and birth of new members. She could not have been an exception to it. She finally accepted her child's death."

All I could understand was that death would happen to each one of us someday but I wondered if knowledge about death also equated to enlightenment. Did learning about death mean learning about life? Thoughts ran incessantly in my mind in between my conversation with Zeba. Was she to be reborn again or this birth was a rebirth for her? Had she come to earth to complete some of the remaining years of her last birth and so she was leaving the world much before her face had wrinkles.

"Have I committed some sin, Zeba?"

She was thoroughly perturbed by what I had asked. "What makes you think like that?" she asked.

"My teacher Raashid Kemal says that if we do something wrong, God punishes us through different means. Is he punishing me for any of my sins by taking you away from me?"

"No, you are a child of God, how can you commit any sin? There are people who are born and live long and there are some who die in the mother's womb, but whether it's a life of one day or one year or hundreds of years, we develop a bond with these souls even if they survive only for a while. The almighty has his own ways of teaching us how to surrender to his will," she replied.

During the last few days of Zeba's life, I had evolved manifold. From initial reaction of anger, I had moved on to guilt and then to the wisdom that decisions of life and death did not lie in the hands of humans. All these years Zeba had talked to me about uncertainties in life and that our destinies were designed and executed by God. But I had finally found one thing that was certain, that in every lifetime, eventually we must die. Our beliefs in the cycle of rebirths, reincarnation, resurrections and transmigration varied with our faiths; every life had to end with death was regardless of that.

11

The Holy Book said we were never to doubt the resurrection; we were created by the almighty from dust. As we see the dry and barren earth, we also witness the rain that moistens the earth and blossoms everything around us. It thus spells out that God is truth and He pours life into the dead and He has power over all things.

If this was true, was Zeba to get resurrected? Was she to come back after the almighty poured life into her? I pondered again.

I turned pages after pages to learn when she would be resurrected and to my disappointment found that resurrection was to happen only on the Day of Judgment. It said that the present life in this world is only an amusement, a time when people compete against one another for greater wealth. This life does not end with death, it continues till the day when people are judged for their virtues and their depravity, each person will have a book containing his/her record of all their deeds. The righteous will receive their books in their right hands and will show their books with pride to each other. The wicked will receive their books in their left hands. And each will say: "I wish this book was not given to me; I wish that I knew nothing about this book; I wish that death had ended my existence.

My thoughts wandered from that book to *Ketaab-e-Hayaat* that Daniyaal had given me. I was a little confused, so I thought I may find the difference in *the Ketaab-e-Hayaat* itself, and I walked to my secret case to bring it out.

Just then I heard a deep voice calling for me.

"Come, Khuda," said Zeba, extending her arm to caress me.

Nothing distressed the quietness of our little hut, save the prattle of birds that flew across the windows. Their sound was always welcoming and we both liked to observe the habits of the birds that sometimes made delicate nests around the left hand corner of the window panes. Cats and dogs also arrived to create some commotion sometimes, however, that day we were blessed with the silence that both of us much needed.

"I had always wanted to tell you about a place where I wanted to go."

"Which place?"

Zeba was that saint in my life as well as in the lives of many others whom she reached out to without any self-interest, but telling it to her in so many words was not what my mind could configure at that age, I could not articulate everything that I sensed.

"The earth has been blessed by people of devotion and virtue. So many of them have been born, lived and have turned this world into a place worth living. They shared the vibrations which reach us and generate a sense of devotion and thankfulness in us. Million journeys are made every day in search of these vibrations" she continued.

Zeba had often spoken to me about the acts of faith, but what she was referring to was not so simple for me to visualize. She was referring to the vibrations that I was living with in her presence; she was my shelter, the source of my inspiration and happiness. I needed no explanation about the state of consciousness or dreams or trance that I was into. Very early in life I had entered the spiritual world and it was none other than she who had held my hand and walked me into it, just that I was to gradually become aware of that path.

"The universe has awesome powers, it gives us life and it nurtures, but it has been kind enough to create souls with the same awesome powers that have given back much more to it. Their consciousness radiates much more light and energy than the world asks for, it is this very light that guides us effortlessly" she said

"But can the souls radiate light after they die?" I was still thinking of death.

"Enlightened souls never die!" she exclaimed

"Within one life, all of us live two different lives Khuda, the inner life and the outer life. Our inner life is filled with silence and we alone deal with it and enjoy it. It deals with thoughts and vibrations that we sense from all the things that we see and feel around us. Though eternal in nature, only the mindful and meditative souls who look through and dwell into their inner life are able to achieve the peace it generates. The outer life brings in a lot of experiences that are material and palpable leading to delight and enjoyment. The irony of living two lives together is fascinating. We start experiencing everything after we are born and seek as much pleasure as possible from the external world but there comes a time when we want to part from it and seek peace which we are unable to experience through the physical world around us. The art of balancing lives and transiting from one to the other has been mastered by enlightened minds alone"

She took a deep breath and continued, "Our inner life is graced with vibrations and gives us spiritual depth. It lays hidden. We often see our outer life growing materially and

Benazir Patil

decaying naturally, culminating in death and we conclude that everything about our life ends there. But as our external life experiences the growth of our physical bodies, our inner life experiences the growth of our mind."

"What are vibrations, Zeba? Are they sounds? Can we hear them?" I asked.

"Vibrations are thoughts that move out from our minds into circles; words are nothing but neatly woven thoughts. In early ages, men sang like birds and created music, the music created vibrations and they could communicate through this music. Perceiving vibrations becomes difficult for those who are unable to understand their inner lives, because they get chained by the events and experiences of the external world around them. At times, animals and plants are more receptive to these vibrations than humans."

While I was talking to Zeba, I was feeling the vibrations. She wanted to tell me something that was very important for her and was connected so strongly to her life. Her energy levels were depleting with every passing moment, dark circles had encircled her beautiful eyes, talking continuously was becoming cumbersome, she was gasping, but I did not want to stop her from talking, my greed for listening to her was increasing as much as her energy was decreasing.

"The devout souls are gifted with the ability to spread their blessedness in every place they pass by. The vibrations that they send out from their inner lives have immense powers. One such devout soul lived in Fatehpur in Hindustan, where I was born."

Zeba was talking to me about the Sufis, who, through their vibrations, could connect with humanity and divine equally.

"I want you to go and feel the vibrations that I have experienced in that place. You may have to take halts at about seven destinations to reach there, but whenever you think you can go, you must go there. My parents had lived there in their early years, when I was eight years old; they migrated to Khorasan as traders and settled there till they lost their lives. My mother always told me various stories of this saint who lived in Fatehpur; I always wanted to take you there."

"Why? Does anybody live there now?" I asked her.

"No, not to meet anybody, but to imbibe the lessons of healing," she said.

I had no clue what healing meant. I just understood that she was talking to me of some spiritual ways she wanted me to learn.

"What lessons?" I asked.

"Everything in the universe is operational through some energy. Everything that you can see and not see is made up of vibrating energy. It was only when I could assimilate this energy in me that I could realize that God had gifted me with the power to heal others!"

"Power to heal? Are you talking of the same powers that *Isa* had?" I asked with a startling expression.

"Yes, what *Isa* did was also healing; you will meet other healers in your life and understand it yourself," she said.

"So there are many people like *Isa* in this world?"

"No, not many. In fact, you will meet all kinds of people in your life; you will meet explorers, people who take up challenges; the aspirers, who run for status and perceive their lives based on what others think of them; the succeeders who win and who take up responsibility; the reformers, who work regardless of rewards; the traders, for whom everything is a matter of trade; the givers who are rare and the healers, the rarest of them all."

I didn't much understand these categories, of all the people I had met, the most influential was the giver, Zeba herself who I had seen generously giving away all she had.

"And why is Fatehpur seven destinations away from here," I asked

"I just thought that it could be seven destinations away, I assumed that going to Fatehpur, for you will be like walking on to a *Ziggurat*," she said.

"*Ziggurat*?" I questioned.

"Yes, a *Ziggurat*. It was always a place of worship for ancient people, they always walked up the steps of *Ziggurat*, which they thought were the dwelling place for the gods, these were the platforms that connected heaven and earth; most of these had seven steps to reach the top, the place of God," she said.

I was immensely fascinated; I wanted to go and see a *Ziggurat*: "how would a bridge between heaven and earth look?" I thought.

Seven, by now had started crossing my mind very often. Daniyaal had once explained to me about how *Isa*, at the time of his crucifixion had suffered seven wounds, two in the palms, two in the wrists, two in the feet, and one on the side.

"I promise you that I will go there one day," I said when I found Zeba waiting to hear my inner thoughts.

Her life was concluding. I had never seen her longing for anything; she was as peaceful as ever, with no more longing for life either.

"As I leave this earthly life, I want to give you all the wealth that I earned. Live your life with this and you will never feel deprived of anything," she smiled, pulling me close to her and caressing my head.

"But now, you must give me something off your wealth," she said.

"What?"

"Tell me a nice story that will make me smile."

"Once an old lady came to Prophet Mohammed and said, "Please pray that God admits me to paradise".

"No old women can enter paradise." The poor old woman began to weep.

"Old ladies become youthful and then enter paradise," said the Prophet.

"And then the old woman went back smiling," I said.

Zeba smiled. The divinity in her smile had a tinge of weariness. The certainty of her death was at last ascertained as she took her last breath.

12

Her closed eyes had taken her into an eternal consciousness. She was now a soul who had transformed into a brighter state of being. Holding the invaluable treasure of modest living, serene meditation and heavenly virtues in her lifetime, Zeba had bequeathed me all. I was to preserve them now.

After entombing her into the ribs of Mother Earth, I stood thinking about her as a teacher without teachings, a sage without sermons, and a saint without any ideology; she was the purest of all.

———◆◈◆———

He came forward, put his hand in the side pocket of his beautiful cloak and without saying a word handed over a small book with a cover that had dazzling golden outline. I looked at the book and was enthralled—there was something magical about it.

Before I could even utter a word, Daniyaal asked me to close my eyes and open my palms. He placed the book in my palms and said, "I give this *Ketaab-e-Hayaat* to you, always keep it with you. This will guide you every time you will want to know something about this universe, Khuda, but you must take care that you do not leave it anywhere and should always carry it with you. It has all the knowledge that you may want to know for this one life that you have."

I listened to what Daniyaal said, I had no questions, and I continued to feel mesmerized as the book lay on my palms. Déjà vu! I felt as if this particular act was being repeated, as if Daniyaal had given me this book earlier, as if I had looked at Daniyaal with awe even before and I had asked him what this book was all about in the past. As the scenes started appearing before my eyes, the fog started clearing a little by little, and all of a sudden it occurred to me as if I had dreamt of everything that was happening.

"Have you read this book?" I asked him.

"Yes, not just me, all of us do, throughout our lives."

"But I have never seen this book with Zeba," I said, consoling my memory.

"She may have it, or she may not have it in the form that you have it in," he said.

"How could a book not be in the form of a book?" This confused me further. I could never sit still with doubts in my mind and always asking questions then and there. It was much later when I had matured into a lad I was gifted with an understanding that all questions could not be and will not be answered immediately; certain questions were to be left unanswered until destiny helped answer them at the right time.

"And do you also have a *Ketaab-e-Hayaat* with you," I asked.

"Yes, I do, but I have been asked to seal the book until the time of the end, when many will rush here and there, and knowledge will increase," he said.

"Time of the end?"

"The time when many of those who sleep in the dust of the earth shall awake: some shall live forever, some shall be disgraced, a time when the wise shall shine brightly, and those who lead the many to justice shall be like the stars forever, a time when many shall fall away and evil shall increase." He said.

"Oh Daniyaal, please tell me, this is so confusing," I said.

"It is not. All of us are born humans, to different parents, in different places, but we all share the same ether, the same realm, the same waters and the same skies. Just as we share so many similar things, we all are guided by the same milestones, so each one of us is given a *Ketaab-e-Hayaat* by the creator, either in the form of a book as I have given you, or in the form of directions that come to us from our parents, teachers and guides. Sometimes we are gifted with signals that Mother Earth sends us from time to time. In whatever form it comes, it comes from the *Ketaab-e-Hayaat* made for us," he explained.

My *Ketaab-e-Hayaat* looked so new and radiant. I was all set to open it when Daniyaal stopped me.

"Not now, you can read it later, read it only when you need to. From now onwards every time you have questions about life and death, truth and fallacies, anger and fear, happiness and torture, you may turn to this book and you will find your answers."

"This is so complicated!"

"It is not. You will know when to read it and when not to. All of us go through the seven questions of life and that is when you will turn to the *Ketaab-e-Hayaat*."

"And what are those seven questions?"

"These are simple. There will be times when your conscience will be heavy and you will want to know if you are doing the right thing; there will be occasions when you will feel lost and you will need directions; there will be moments when your mind will engage in the act of reflecting on what you have already done. And there will be many such times when you will feel the need to open this book."

"My conscience?"

"Your conscience is your inner chamber where the lamp of the lord continues to burn all the time. This lamp is your guard that throws light on all the deeds that you do. There will be times when your conscience will ask you questions and you will find it difficult to respond. Your *Ketaab-e-Hayaat* will help you understand yourself."

I felt a bit lost. Daniyaal walked me to my home and bid goodbye, promising me to meet the next day.

13

The night approached. I sat quietly reflecting on what Daniyaal had said. I looked and re-looked at the *Ketaab-e-Hayaat*. I could not for long comprehend if Zeba was really no more around me. My eyes kept turning to the small window I normally peeped into to converse with Zeba while she sat on the ground and cooked bread for both of us. It seemed as if she was still doing that. My eyes felt heavy, I had not slept for the last three nights, and I had been by her bedside all the time.

On the previous night Zeba had remembered about Daniyaal, "Have you been meeting your friend of late?"

"Yes Zeba, why?"

"No, nothing, I was just wanting to know if he ever explained anything to you about that wisdom," she enquired.

"Yes, he did. One day I had asked him about what wisdom he wanted to give me. And he had explained that he does not want to give me anything; it is the lord who gives wisdom to the wise. He had told me about the myriad changes: the change from day to night, from one season to another, or a change from youth to old age. All these are governed by a decree established by Him. And so how much ever we deny His existence, He is the only one who gives us all the wisdom and understanding." I said.

"This is all that he has told you?"

"No, he has also told me about dreams and that each dream has an interpretation for sure."

"You mean what we dream is real and that is likely to happen?"

"Yes, the dreams seen in our slumber are certain and they have a meaning to it. Dreams are one of God's ways of communicating with us, and there are mysteries hidden in our dreams."

"So is there any dream that you remember?" she asked.

"Yes, I do."

"But you never told me about it."

"Because, I wondered about it. It was rather strange!"

"What was it?"

"I could see myself walking endlessly into some lonely fields, tired and thirsty, almost about to fall. Suddenly, from somewhere I see a man walking towards me—he also seemed to have walked from far to reach me. He was old, with wrinkles galore, but his eyes shimmered with joy, as if he had achieved something unusual."

"Where are you going?" he asked me.

"Nowhere."

"But you have been walking for so long."

"Even you look tired, as if you have walked a long way."

"Yes, indeed, I have walked from a long distance to tell you something important."

"What is that?"

"The man with three heads has been waiting for you; you should go and meet him."

"Man with three heads? Who?"

"Yes, there is one."

He uttered these words and walked ahead. In no time he had disappeared. I wondered what he had meant by this. How and where I could find a man with three heads, I asked myself and then I woke up to understand that I was dreaming" I told Zeba.

"Everything in life happens at the right time, so perhaps you may also meet this man when it is time for you to meet him. It is no mystery, keep patience and be watchful," she consoled me.

I finally fell asleep. The next morning, I awoke sensing that I was to begin a different life, not of loneliness . . . but of a purpose . . .

The time had come, I thought. I opened my secret chest and brought out my precious *Ketaab-e-Hayaat*. I opened a page randomly as Daniyaal had instructed. I went to Page 52, it read:

The birds of the world came together; to search for their king

The hoopoe told them, there is one, the Simorgh, who lives far away in distant lands and to meet him, a journey to those lands was to be made

The 7th Destination

Enthusiastically the birds agreed, then realized the difficulties of a long journey

The nightingale, the lover, said he cannot leave his beloved; the hawk said he had to wait at the court; the finch, the coward, feared to fly out to new lands; the parrot said he was caged and could not be disloyal; the peacock said he had to wait for someone to show his way back to paradise; the duck said he could not leave the waters and go in deserts and give up his purity; the partridge said he could not leave the pearl; the Homayoun said he had to wait for the kings; the heron said he needs to wait for the buried gold.

Many fears and many desires; the hoopoe counselled them on their desires and fears.

The birds left, flew a little, but raised numerous questions about the way forward.

They were frightened by the emptiness of the path.

And the Hoopoe responded:
"Consume your life with prayer till Solomon Bestows his glance and ignorance is gone. When Solomon accepts you, you will know far more than my unequal words can show."

They wonder what gift they should ask for from the Simorgh.

And the Hoopoe responded:
"Poor fool, make one request: Seek only Him, of all things He is best; If you're aware of Him, in all the earth, what could you wish for of a greater worth? Whoever joins Him in that secret place is step by step admitted to His grace."

Many questions they asked, Hoopoe answered all, the last one being about the length of journey.

And the Hoopoe responded:
"Before we reach our goal, the journey's seven valleys lie ahead;

>The first stage is the Valley of the Quest;
>Then Love's wide valley is our second test;
>The third is Insight into Mystery;
>The fourth Detachment and Serenity;
>The fifth is Unity;
>The sixth is Awe, a deep Bewilderment unknown before;
>The seventh Poverty and Nothingness.

The birds asked Hoopoe how he knows about the seven valleys!

And the Hoopoe responded:
"Solomon has glanced at me; the glance which is worth far more than prayer. Unceasingly one should pray until Solomon glances at one."

The journey takes them through the seven valleys: of quest, love, understanding, detachment, unity, astonishment, and finally poverty and nothingness.

The valley of the quest is filled with difficulties and trials; they are tested and become free.

In the valley of love they learn that love has nothing to do with reason.

The valley of understanding teaches that knowledge is temporary, but understanding endures. Overcoming faults and weaknesses brings the seeker closer to the goal.

In the valley of independence and detachment one has neither a desire to possess nor a wish to discover. To cross this difficult *valley one must be roused from apathy to renounce inner and outer attachments so that one can become self-sufficient.*

In the valley of unity the Hoopoe announces that although you may see many beings, in reality there is only one, which is complete in its unity. As long as you are separate, good and evil will arise; but when you lose yourself in the divine essence, they will be transcended by love.

When unity is achieved, one forgets all and forgets oneself in the valley of astonishment and bewilderment.

The Hoopoe declares that the last valley of deprivation and death is almost impossible to describe. In the immensity of the divine ocean the pattern of the present world and the future world dissolves. As you realize that the individual self does not really exist, the drop becomes part of the great ocean forever in peace.

The journey is dealt with and the birds arrive at the court of the Simorgh.

And they found that the Simorgh they sought was none other than themselves.

Out of thousands of birds only thirty reach the end of the journey. Simorgh, it turns out, means thirty birds;

By annihilating themselves gloriously in the Simorgh they find themselves in joy, learn the secrets, and receive immortality.

They learn, as long as you do not realize your nothingness and do not renounce your self-pride, vanity, and self-love, you will not reach the heights of immortality.

They reach the goal of their quest.

Benazir Patil

14

Sadness had not yet seeped in. Zeba's departure had led me to a *parwaaz*, a flight as glorious and unimaginable as a raven's. I was springing into a magnificent but mysterious universe. I did not care for what I was sowing or reaping, neither did I plan for a storehouse or a barn. A streak of radiance was being painted on the canvas of my life as I continued from one voyage to the other. All my fourteen years with Zeba were measured by the countless moments of love, happiness and compassion; the songs of life that she taught me were to remain with me forever.

"Kindness of the earth will teach you silence, patience; you will learn from her love; misery and hardship you will triumph by all the strength she transmits to you, so continue with your journey. Do not stop till you have reached infinity," were her last words.

I had no clue if I was to depart in search of a solitary monastery or explore a universe filled with relationships. The only certainty I knew of was that it would be akin to a pilgrimage. On the threshold of my youth, the chance to create a delightful dream almost awaited me; I could search for teachers in nature and take pride in my heritage that inspired me to honor humility.

Having set the rules for myself, I decided to walk ahead with seven companions Zeba had left me with: humanity, freedom, justice, truth, patience, strength and love. Living with these meant:

I was to endorse humanity and never be inhuman to others.
I was to uphold freedom and never to patronize any kind of subjugation.
I was to be just and righteous and never to support injustice.
I was to follow the truth and never to let the untruth triumph.
I was to live with patience and never to get frustrated.
I was to display strength and never be meek.
I was to spread love and reduce the hatred from this world.

Without thinking too hard I had entered this simple and beautiful life. A life that was to lead me to a path on which I would visit places, meet the poor and the rich and learn from the worldly and the mystics, shed tears of joy and sorrow and understand life and death. The mystery of life and death had however started unfolding itself much before I asked for it. Zeba had rightly spelt out that the body departs but the soul remains. I had been mentally talking to her about my newfound evolution.

Life after death was being revealed to me more explicitly by the *Ketaab-e-Hayaat*. It referred to the scriptures that so triumphantly stated different laws by which people lived for many centuries.

The first law of existence stated about the rising of the humans after death into a form of which we may not have the slightest knowledge.

The second law spelt out the realities of God's first creation and the second that were to be absolutely identical.

The third law emphasized how absence from the body meant presence with the lord.

The fourth law identified how the good and evil that happened in our present life was a result of the good or bad

Benazir Patil

deeds from a previous life. The good and the bad deeds committed in the present life were to determine all good and evil that was to take place in the next life.

The fifth one proclaimed, in all of us there lives an embodied soul that is enslaved by *maya*, the illusion, and which can only be purified after it has freed itself from all worldly desires.

The sixth one clarified, each soul is responsible for its own predicament as well as its own salvation; hence, a soul may transmigrate from one life form to another for countless of years, taking with it the *karma* that it has earned until it finds conditions that produce the needed fruits.

The seventh law emphatically stated the clash between microcosm and macrocosm—the communication between the diverse parts of a human being with those of the universe that incessantly sought to define a unity between the humans and the physical world.

But all upheld the truth that there was nothing in the universe that could die; everything will renew and continue to live.

One day, while I sat contemplating on all these matters, something inspired me to open the *Ketaab-e-Hayaat,* on Page 124, it read:

> *The body of mankind is an illustration of the material world. For the world is made out of a drop of water. Men too are coming into being out of a drop of water.*
>
> *Just as the width of the world is equal to its length, man's too is likewise. And every person has his own length and width. The human body resembles seven elements of the universe and encloses a treasure of similarities.*

Our skin is like the sky
Our flesh is like earth
Our bones are like mountains
Our veins are like rivers
Out blood is like the water of the sea
Our belly is like the ocean
And our hair is like the plants

Though it was that time when the thought of death weighed heavily on my mind, little understanding on the finite nature of our being did not allow me to think past my anxieties. As I began to realize that existence in this life was determined much by what reality humans looked for after death, there were umpteen principles in various scriptures that focused on life after death congruent with deeds performed in this life. The most interesting of all ideologies was the threefold return law of the *Wiccans*: it meant that anything you did to others came back to you with three times the power. So if you did evil to someone, it would happen to you with three times its graveness and, if you extended goodness, you could anticipate just the same happening to you in an enormous way.

Vedic philosophy was equally fascinating: it considered rebirth in every species as per the actions of their soul. The belief that the inclinations of one's souls were carried from one birth to another without any remembrance encouraged them to pray for healthy eyes and intellect for the next birth. It asked for a pure mind to conduct noble actions so that they come back to the world as human beings. There are two paths for the soul: one path, *Pitriyan*, provides birth again and again through the union of father and mother, good and bad deeds, happiness and sorrow. The other path of *Devayana* frees the soul from the cycle of birth and death and provides bliss of salvation. The whole world reverberates with both these paths after gifting us ultimate bliss or *Mukti*. The bodies were compared to mere garments: just as worn-out garments are shed by the body, worn-out bodies are shed by the dweller within the body. The dweller then dons a new, like garments.

I was trying to understand what those controlling forces behind the events were? My own actions, attitude and behaviours were pushing me to take responsibility of what I was undergoing. But the people I was meeting with and the situations that I was exposed to were external to me. As much as I saw humanity chasing the picture of life after death, I also witnessed them chasing happiness. Despite the fact that people had different goals to follow, there lay an almost common causal objective to nearly all their quests—the goal to be happy. I could see some spending all their time in creating wealth that could suffice for eternity, because only treasures could make them happy. I saw people struggling to possess relationships, assets, abode, and bodies, all for reaching the only goal of being happy. Inexplicably, measuring perfect happiness was as difficult as calculating the deeds required for a perfect afterlife.

I thought little about my afterlife. I was busy concentrating on the present. Wandering from the realms of Hamadan to the villages and towns was not so much of a coincidence; my life was perhaps designed to be like that. Like every other soul, I was busy actualizing the plans that the almighty had chalked out for me. The concepts of destiny, fate or divine approvals were not novel to my mind. While fate got down to telling me about how it unfolded each step of my life, destiny harped on that everything will turn out as it should. 'Pagan', perhaps fitted me as the most apt epithet.

The belief that every event has a cause and that everything in the cosmos was regulated by cosmic laws was gradually building up. But, I could not hold on to it completely—was everything really predetermined? I was dealing with a bearable struggle, I thought. A lot in my life was dependent on what I did; something inside my soul was asking me to do what I was doing. That was not all; it also sent me clear signals when I ventured on a wrong path. Those were solemn tussles, and I realized I could not handle the combined game of destiny and determination. The more I felt that my life was destined to be what it was, my conscience would blow me up by making loud pronouncements that I should be determined to make it what I wanted it to be.

Mother Earth, nevertheless, was on my side, truly manifesting the directions my life could take.

Benazir Patil

For a just man falleth seven times, and riseth up again: but the wicked shall fall into mischief.

Proverbs 24:1

15

The sun was exactly above me. The sweltering breeze hit my face constantly.

I was no more a wanderer to myself; what I was to others was yet to be revealed to me.

A few hours had passed without much deviation. I had reached a spot where the land was barren, sans vegetation sans life. When a child, I was afraid of even imagining being alone in an alien land. However, since the days I started walking alone, a sense of fearlessness had set into me. All of a sudden I realized my horse was feeling unnerved about something. "I needed to feed him perhaps," I told myself. I dismounted and looked around. In the past I had walked to several places but Haroon had encouraged me to go with my horse as the road to Balkh was a little tough.

Both of us needed some rest. Instead it felt like it was a time to pray. I did ablution with mud and began reciting the seven holy verses:

> In the name of Allah, the Most Beneficent, the Most Merciful;
> All praise is due to Allah, Lord of the world;
> The Most Beneficent, the Most Merciful;
> The Lord of the Day of Judgement;
> Thee alone do we worship and Thee alone we seek for help;
> Guide us to the Right Path.

As I finished praying and looked at the horse, I sensed the string tied on my arm. The talisman, I always knew of, but nobody knew who had tied it for me. Neither Zeba mentioned, nor I ever asked her. All I knew was that a paper with seven verses from Yasin written on it was rolled and kept in the hollow space. All seven ended with the word 'Mobin', meaning something that is clear by itself and is far in resemblance to anything else. The Quran they said is 'Mobin'. Clear in its content, it clarifies truth from falsehood, guidance from misguidance, and the believers from the disbelievers. Above all, it clarifies the mind of a person.

I once again prostrated to Mother Earth and quietly listened to her.

"Go climb the pyramid of your life." the sound resonated in my ears as if Mother Earth was making some heavenly proclamation. I opened my eyes and lifted them to look around. Strangely, there were no pyramids.

I wondered if once upon a time, there were pyramids there. "The pyramids," Arabs wrote, "faced numerous disasters; many of them collapsed and were rebuilt." What attracted my interest was that most pyramids had seven steps, and though it appeared to be a triangle, it was also a square. There was something esoteric about it. These were actually tombs of kings and queens and covered the bodies of the dead, but why were they ladder like? Perhaps they were symbols of ascension, walking upwards to the point at the head of the edifice. I had to understand the deeper sense it revealed. Why had Mother Earth asked me to climb the pyramid of my life? Was it something to do with my death or was it about those seven steps? It was about climbing, but the thought of entering that cosmic cave was equally intriguing.

My thoughts drove me to silence, as if I was to live with the aura of inexpressibility. An existence of this sort was still unimaginable to me.

Yazd had already housed me in its environs for three long years. Though I had made a few friends in the town, I was not as popular with them as with small children who often gathered around me to listen to stories of the ancient world. Narrating my childhood incidents was a ritual they adored. So much so that the children insisted I become their teacher in their school and they found their teachers absolutely monotonous. But I was happy with the work that I was doing, I was not sure, if ever I would have loved to be a teacher, at least at that time I was not.

After having lived in Hamadan for fourteen years, Yazd was too large a town for my imaginations, with large streets and burgeoning industries. With no riches loaded on me, Haroon, my newfound friend had gathered on day one through my talks that I owned nothing and would need some work to sustain myself.

The natives often narrated the changing scenes of the old city growing into new. Rich and unique in its architecture, it was a cauldron of several cultures. It was not the silk or just the cultural dwellings that made the city look different to me; a blend of languages along with thin layers of residents from multiple religions between the deserts of 'Dasht-e-Kavir' and 'Dasht-e-Lut', one after the other, had actually turned it into an oasis.

"One morning," I started narrating a story to my little friends . . .

". . . When I was walking back home, I saw a huge crowd near a poor man's dwelling. A rich man stood just outside auctioning the belongings from the house. After asking some people I could identify the poor labourer standing in one corner with complete meekness as he listened to the huge crowd betting prices and taking away whatever little he had.

That troubled me. Agitated I ran to Zeba to share what I had seen."

"Zeba?"

"My Mother!"

"She made every effort to explain to me that this was because the poor man had not been able to repay the loan that he may have taken from the rich businessman; she explained how the poor fall into the trap of borrowing from the rich moneylenders and how the power to control their lives is assumed and used by the corrupt minds of the moneylenders. But all her efforts were in vain. I was in no state of mind to understand why the rich man had no other resort but to sell off the poor man's belongings which were so meager."

"It was all so inhuman, is money making, becoming rich makes you behave like a criminal? Are riches a blessing of god or is it something that can be earned only through exploiting the poor?"

"Possessing wealth is not wrong; sometimes God blesses you with it even if you do not crave for it. When you have wealth and still live humbly, then you are on the right path, then you are just a messenger of god in helping others, but earning wealth by exploiting others, especially the poor, digresses you from the path of god. Khuda, my grandfather, would tell me a story of a wealthy man who lay on his deathbed. All his life he had accumulated money and riches. As he was dying he thought that perhaps in his afterlife too he would need money to buy things, so he told his sons to put a bag of gold coins inside the coffin along with his body when they bury him after his death."

With immense inquisitiveness and innocence I asked her, "Oh, can we carry our wealth with us to heaven also after we die?"

"Wait! Listen to what happened after that. His last wish was fulfilled by his sons. When he entered the next world it took the angels a long time to trace his name in any of the good books of god, so much so that he became hungry and thirsty waiting there while they were busy looking for his name in the list of good deeds. He waited and waited and then walked to a place nearby and found some people eating wonderful meals. He told those people to give him food extending the money he had brought with him. He was told that the money he had brought had no worth in heaven and they used different means to buy things. They told him that he would get the food against all the wealth he had given away to the needy during his lifetime. The man tried hard but could not recall giving away any such wealth while he lived."

"The angel standing next to the man told him: 'what you spent on you was yours, what you kept with you got lost, and what you gave away is what you will get back today" "said Zeba.

"So what we earn and collect and possess in this life is not really ours Khuda, it is only what we give away to the needy is given back to us in the world of god," she added.

"How does God decide how many people should be living in this world?" One of the children asked me astonishingly.

"Perhaps after making the first set of human beings, god kept replacing those who died with birth of new children and may be that is how we all were born. His calculations must have been influenced by his belief that there should be sufficient souls to take care of everything that he had created," I responded with a smile.

"Does God have time to listen to what we are talking?" asked Ejaaz.

"Is it not impossible for Him to listen to so many of us, how does he manage to listen to our prayers?" added Afshan.

Some even questioned God's intentions of sending so many people to this world and felt that it was precisely the reason why so many people were born poor and did not have enough to eat. Thinking of all this as a child was certainly appropriate; a variation leading to maturity in these thoughts was very likely, but in my case perhaps, I continued to think likewise even after growing up.

My experience had taught me that it was difficult for the small minds to fathom the meaning of natural decrees established by the Supreme. Evolution of mind is a natural process for humankind. I was also evolving, trying to reach somewhere in my understanding. Reaching the final stage of evolution would take years, I contemplated, but was man capable of understanding what that final stage was? I asked myself.

Whether or not I believed in the existence of god and understood His various names that I was getting introduced to, every new incident exploded a question into my senses. I began to realize that there prevailed some 'design', some arrangement for mankind, with some direction for human evolution to proceed with. This was no secret design as many Gnostics talked about it and displayed it as some mysterious knowledge. Whatever mankind was doing in the universe either had a good or a harmful effect on it, so either they followed the directions and evolved or retreated back to stages where they were ages ago.

I was quite intrigued by what the *dervishes* spoke, about the 'real self' and the 'false self'. It was complicated for me to understand. The *Ketaab-e-Hayaat* was teaching me that we all possessed intellect, but we were rarely governed by it, because continuous thoughts, distinct emotions and various instincts made us do what we would not do if we followed our intellect alone.

I very much wanted to understand what this 'true self' really was? I was incessantly interacting with different faiths burgeoning around me. The philosophies disseminated by each of those were not the real worry. The interpretations, its followers forced upon their fellow beings, indeed were. Faiths were no more being practised and followed; they were being distributed, spoken about and becoming the basis for mayhem. I was living in a century where people searched for justifications for their acts in the name of god; the aspects of goodness and holiness were being maneuvered to suit each one's life. Though every faith just focused on serving humanity, its analysis merely meant that humanity had its own fences. Living by any faith required serving god on earth in order to live with Him forever in heaven but what did it mean by serving god was pathetically literal. The god either stood on the pedestal, in temples and churches or was a formless entity that everyone was paying obeisance to. 'Reaching out to fellow beings was a means to reach the almighty' was rarely a concern.

The thoughts were simply mounting on my mind. I opened the *Ketaab-e-Hayaat*, Page 34, and it read:

> *Syad-asti: may be, it is;*
> *Syad-nasti: may be, it is not;*
> *Syad-asti-nasti ca: may be, it is and it is not;*
> *Syad-avaktavyah: may be, it is indeterminate;*

Syad-asti sca, avaktavyah sca: may be, it is and is indeterminate;
Syad-nasti sca, avaktavyah sca: may be, it is not and also
indeterminate and;
Syad-asti-nasti sca, avaktavyah sca: may be, it is and it is not
and also indeterminate.

Things exist and things do not. Any reality has several
possibilities, it is seven ways of predication that give us
sufficient explanation of it, says Syadvada.

Syadvada searches for the meaning of things from all probable
perspectives. Anything and everything is subject to limitations
imposed by objective differences of substance, time, space and
attributes. According to a Jaina all judgements are relative
and true under certain conditions. Each one of these seven
alternatives holds good.

This was strange; a thought to an understanding of this kind
was beyond my comprehension. I marked the page and decided
to return to it some other day.

16

I was busy celebrating *Shab-e-Yalda* in the alley. The ceremony on winter solstice was meant to celebrate the birthday of Sun, an important event of the ancient Iranian religion that symbolized the victory of Light and Good against Darkness and Evil. The very fact that from this day onwards, days would grow longer and give more light conceptualized the triumph of light over darkness.

The bonfires were lit outside, and I sat around the *korsi* filled with fruit and vegetables from Haroon's house. I was interacting with his father for the first time; before that I had only spoken to him about a few things at work. He asked me if it was my first time in Yazd. I told him that I had only heard about the town and its magnificent buildings from Daniyaal and had never been there before.

I expressed to him about my last visit to Raashid's house at the time of *Nowroz*. "Though I had celebrated it in Hamadan too, I had for the first time explored the ritual and the festivities that laid out *haft sin*. *Sabzeh* was a symbol of rebirth; *Samanu*, a symbol of affluence; *Senjed*, a symbol of love; *Sir*, a symbol of medicine; *Sib*, a symbol of beauty and health; *Somaq*, a symbol of the sunrise; and *Serkeh*, a symbol of age and patience," I told Haroon.

"So are the rituals of *Yalda*. A common practice is about engaged youths sending a platter of seven different fruit to their fiancées along with myriad gifts. It is also a night of magic," he responded.

Yazd had woken me up in *Zarthosht's* world. My curiosity to know about him remained kindled for years, but the quest had got re-kindled and burned as much as the flame that I saw in the temple where Haroon had taken me. It had been burning for about fifteen hundred years.

"When *Zarthosht* turned seven, some men tried to kill him through black magic," Haroon's father Imran said to me. "But as he turned fifteen, he submitted himself voluntarily to religion and in another five years left his home. He started living in a cave located on one of the mountains. He spent seven long years meditating in the cave and attained enlightenment. He felt that it was time for him to reach out and teach the world about the righteousness and guidance of Ahura Mazda."

"What knowledge did he want to spread?" I asked him.

"Not much is known about that age, it was perhaps many years before Christ. It is heard that he had a vision, *Vohu Manah* appeared before him and asked him to declare the Good News to the world."

"Vohu Manah?"

"Yes, *Vohu Manah*, one of the seven great emanations of Ahura Mazda, the one Wise Lord, means good mind or good thinking. The virtue of good thinking, or reason, is a divine gift to human beings, and every time we use our reason and our intellectual abilities, we are using our *Vohu Manah*. *Zarthosht*, while presenting his revelation, invited his listeners to think about what he said and reason it out for themselves before they accepted it. *Vohu Manah* is one of the ways that God communicates with us—through the use of our reason. Whenever we use our *Vohu Manah*, we are actually entering into communion with God. Through *Vohu*

Manah come our best ideas, our inspirations, and our finer thoughts." he responded.

"This is amazing, and what was the Good News that he declared to the world?"

"As the first prophet of the world, he brought home the message that one can only worship one God!" said Imran.

"He revealed about the judgment after death; the punishment of sins and reward for good deeds; and the Savior who would come at the End of Time, born of a virgin mother, the reason for the everlasting flame is all about that. He identified the almighty with radiance and light and the persistent burning of the flame is a symbol of uninterrupted light," he said.

"Is the religion of *Zarthosht* the original religion of Iran?" I asked, subtly realizing that I perturbed the gentleman, but his kindness gave way to my anthropological need.

"Yes, it was," he responded without hesitation and added: "It is only recently that the people in our country are realizing and trying to dig out their antiquity."

"Why do you feel so?" I asked him with some doubts.

"You are asking me to respond to a very difficult question, my son," he said and pondered over my expressions.

"All of us know that we had an indigenous religion and culture of our own which survives not only in books but also in our hearts."

His honest disclosure made my eyes numb. In the world where people were fighting over trivialities of religion and sects, here was a man who could sense the depth of his heart and gather the courage to speak about it.

"What according to you was so special about this religion?"

"This religion is also called 'Worship of Wisdom', and the philosophy is very simple: it asks you to dwell in 'Good Thoughts, Good Words and Good Deeds;' it explains life as nothing but a battlefield of moral and immoral forces, the belief that Good prevails over Evil and that humans possess the power to do so is very prominent."

"Is not this very similar to Islam and Christianity?" I asked.

"Yes, indeed, but *Zarthosht's* religion does not ask you to worship alone; it encourages you to transform and progress. The very symbol 'fire' signifies that."

"How?" Curiosity engulfed me completely.

"Fire is the only element that defies gravity; you can see it moving upwards, never downwards."

Amazed at his understanding, my mind got tempted to reach for the *Ketaab-e-Hayaat*—I needed some wisdom on the ways of life *Zarthosht* had recommended.

I often met with *Zarthoshtis* who were involved either in commerce or agriculture. Truthful and hardworking, they were always hired by many businessmen in Yazd. Yet, despite all the good qualities, they were not looked up to, but were considered pagans and people of the lowest order of humanity. Suffering immense insults, they continued to live in the not-so-good world. Yazd gave them more refuge than any other place in the vicinity in the burgeoning Islamic world around them. At times, the misery was at its ultimate and countless of them accepted conversion so as to lead calm and reputable existence. Ironically enough, *Zarthosht* had said "Promotion of life and happiness is the means through which evil will eventually be eradicated from the world."

My curiosity knew no bounds. I was hearing about all of this for the first time. I was reminded of Daniyaal; he had told me about his meetings with different cultures that he discovered during his journeys. This was so true about my journeys too.

As I got tempted to ask more questions to Imran, Haroon interrupted our conversation and in the midst of all the festivities took me aside. He seemed to be somewhat distressed about something. I always found him naïve and acted like an elder brother to him.

"Are you clear what you want in life," asked Haroon.

He was a companion to me in the shop I worked in Yazd, a helpful soul like him had even helped me to find a place for comfortable stay in the vicinity of my work place. Haroon was a brother of two sisters and lived with his parents who were soon getting old. He was leading a life with great ambitions and dreams. I respected him for his integrity. I think everybody did; the businessman we worked for always reflected about him to all others, that to earn his trust, they should work like Haroon.

I was not sure if I was aiming at achieving something at that age or what I was heading towards. I had to tell the truth to Haroon, I was not to live there forever and was to move for my onward journey to Fatehpur. In some ways I was clear about what I wanted in life.

"I follow my own beliefs and I create a harmony in my life through what I feel like doing, without ever regretting for what I have done and not done," I responded with a smile.

"That is so vague, do you know what you are doing and what you plan to achieve in life?"

"Yes, I know about it Haroon. If you try and create music with just one note, it may not happen; it has to be a harmonious blend of seven notes in an octave. The harmony and rhythm of one's life has to be a combination of many things that one is exposed to in life; intellect alone cannot guide to harmony. Truth, courage, emotions, hard work, and many others also surge together to guide where one wants to go and where one aims to reach. But one thing about these notes is worth remembering: when we use the eighth note, we go back to start all over again and move on to the seven notes again," I smiled and said.

"Why do you tell me such weird things; how does one decide which direction to follow Khuda?"

Though I knew that I was to actually help Haroon in disentangling the cobwebs thriving inside him, I often led him to think more.

"What do I tell you about the directions? Our lives run in circles. We are supposed to travel in all the directions, only then can we grow spiritually, emotionally, physically and mentally."

"I have no clue what you are talking about?" said he.

"We all know of four different directions that we see around us," I started.

"Yes, but I am not talking of these directions Khuda. I want to understand the direction where life carries me to achieve some success. The last few years have been difficult. I have seen my father struggling so much just to earn his livelihood and looking after the family has been a burden for him, that is why I decided to leave everything and work to earn a living so that I help him in some ways. I wonder if I am walking in the right direction!"

"East is the direction from where the sun rises. The rising sun is a ray of hope, a direction in our lives where our spirits rise high." I could see Haroon gaining some interest in my talks gradually.

"West is the direction from where we receive our healing; south is the direction that teaches us about love and emotion and helps us get the courage to face our fears; North gives us wisdom and teaches us about sacrifice."

"So all four directions teach us something? Is that what you are saying?" he asked.

"Yes, the direction above is the fifth one, the sky, like a father watching over us, gives us a clear vision; and the direction below us is green, is our Mother Earth that gives us everything and takes care of us."

"So we have two more directions to look at."

"Yes, and the seventh one lies within us. A great spirit lies inside of us, it is that sacred existence inside us, without which nothing else can work, run, live or exist."

With this I asked him to kneel down on the ground and prostrate.

"You want me to thank the almighty?" he asked me.

"I want you to sense quietly the vibrations Mother Earth is extending."

He obeyed me without any hesitation just as Zeba had done. Other than her Haroon was the first person I was teaching the act of listening to Mother Earth.

"I am feeling as if something in me has got revived," he said, waking up from the *Sajdah*.

"Do not explain anything, just practise it more often; you will know more about yourself and the world around you from Mother Earth," I said.

Before Haroon could ask me more questions I signalled to him that I needed to leave.

With a tired body, I entered the house, but my mind was as fresh as ever and wanted to grasp some insights from the *Ketaab-e-Hayaat*.

I opened it, Page 133 read:

> *Seven Buddhist treasures and seven deities of good luck reside in the far off land of Japan, people believe that they reincarnate seven times, and they also mourn for seven weeks after death.*
>
> *Shichi (seven) fuku (luck) jin (beings) are deities since the Edo period. They are often seen on their treasure ship (takara-bune).*
>
> *Ebisu: the patron of fishermen, he ensures safe journeys for all, is a guardian of the rice fields and agriculture, and blesses*

people with prosperity in return for their hard work. His symbol is a large fish.

Daikoku: the incarnation of Shiva, he protects people against evil forces and ensures wealth in commerce and trade. He is a guardian of cooks.

Benten: an angel of Sarasvati. She is the goddess of luck and love; her virtues include happiness and longevity. She sits on a lotus leaf, and sometimes rides a white dragon, sea serpent or snake.

Fukurokuju: renowned for performing miracles, is the deity of wisdom and longevity. He holds a sturdy walking stick to support himself in his advancing years. On the walking stick is tied a parchment scroll (makimono) on which is written sacred teachings and all the wisdom of the world.

Hotei: thought to be the reincarnation of Maitreya, is a god of abundance and laughter. He carries a ceremonial fan and a large bag of riches over his shoulder.

Jurojin: a Taoist god, who carries a scroll that contains a life study of the world and the secrets for longevity.

Bishamon: a Buddhist deity, is a protector of the righteous and a symbol of authority. He lives in the earth's core at the fourth layer, carries a small 'treasure tower' in his left hand. He is the god of war and patron of warriors and the defender of peace.

17

"Let your heart open up," he said.

"What is my work? I am not here to explain to you anything; I am neither a teacher nor any avatar, just a human being like you all who is also evolving with passing years. What we are not doing is opening up our hearts and welcoming everything that god is giving us, whether it is experiences, feelings or mere lessons."

I was tempted to tell him that I had read about this in the *Ketaab-e-Hayaat* long ago, but I didn't. Instead, I said, "I also feel that opening up our hearts to the world around us helps us in understanding the riddle of our presence and birth."

"Can you explain how? To make your friends understand better," he asked me immediately.

"When we receive joy we feel glorified; when we receive lessons that are laden with misery, we curse our creator, instead of understanding the reality that adverse things occur only to guide us, we reject all of that. But as we open up our hearts we realize the message that comes with starving and feasting, silence and discourse, melancholy and cheer."

He was not astonished by what I had mentioned, but he looked at me as if I was made of a different material. What I had said had triggered his exclusive attention at me and it seemed as if he wanted to converse more.

"As we grow, several questions keep coming up," he said.

"The questions about why we exist? Who we are? From where have we come? What is our purpose? Why do we desire what we do? Why do we dream? What lies inside us? Do we really have a mind that can think? How can we be true human beings? What is this universe? Who is managing it? And how do we find answers to all of this?" he asked us.

I had been searching for these answers for long and had realized that we get these answers through the events of life as they occur from time to time. But I refrained from sharing it with the group, not that I was ever conscious about anything, hearing more from others was equally an event I thought.

Baba Shahryaar had been in Balkh for years. People from earlier generations talked about his efforts to reach out to the needy and the distressed, he was a hermit with an attitude of a labourer. People affectionately revered him as 'Shah Baba'. A *dervish* though, he never advocated any doctrine, he just talked about reasoning, goodness and love. My interactions with him had awakened a *dervish* inside me, a strange feeling was exploding; I felt as if I was not the same Khudabakhsh and did not belong to this world. I thought Shah Baba was me and I was him. Many people looked at my wandering as a motive to search some invaluable treasure. I wondered if people like me and Shah Baba were considered purposeless vagabonds—we certainly weren't ones.

In the midst of all these thoughts I asked him "Do you enjoy the life that you are leading now?"

"What kind of life?" he asked.

"Life of a recluse."

"Are we all not leading a similar kind of life? We all are as much a recluse as much as we are befrienders, the worldly people," he responded.

"Our entire life is like a stream that keeps on moving in the mid of two counterparts, the difficulty arises when we look at just one part and ignore the other. Optimism and pessimism coincide and become a powerful strength, but we find it difficult to accept their co-existence in our minds. Sometimes we have the inclination to isolate ourselves and leave this world, but just when we are doing it, we miss the world around us and want to come back to the hubbub we were running away from," he paused and continued as he saw me listening to him with deep reflection.

"We become slaves of our reactions to the external world, our thoughts do not remain ours, we just respond to what we see outside of us, our anger is but a reaction to something we have seen, felt and disliked, and our sadness creeps in as our wants remain unfulfilled." He stopped at that.

"You mean, we long to live like hermits but we find it difficult to do so?" I questioned.

"Yes, we get caged by countless sentiments. Everything that happens in our lives is judged by what we have been conditioned with; we see ourselves doing something good and we love us for that, and we see ourselves doing something wrong and we despise our entire being. We are dealing constantly with the opposites inside us: opposite emotions, opposite thoughts and opposite energies." He paused and continued.

"To comprehend the creation, we have to recognize ourselves first without any deduction and assumptions about ourselves. It is just the same when it comes to comprehending the aspects that are external to us. When we are happy, we are

Benazir Patil

oblivious to all the pain we have been through and when we are in crisis, we are never reminded of happiness, whether inside or outside. We find it difficult to balance ourselves with these opposites."

Shah Baba's contemplations had made me pensive. I had myriad questions to ask, but I decided to think more: it was premature to put him through the quests on which I had not worked myself. I let him continue.

"We live with incomplete visualizations. The inability to visualize things in completion is not a mistake, but understanding partial reality does lead to ignorance, so we have to see things in its entirety and completeness," he said.

I pondered over his words. A man with no possessions, leading an unburdened life, had never been tired of living. 'Shahryaar', meaning 'King', was truly a king of devoutness, for a moment he appeared to be a sorcerer of the stories that I had heard from Zeba, and the very next moment, he came across as an embodiment of a loving and loyal animal that had semblance with the fairy tales from my childhood.

Suddenly, I felt that the child inside me had grown into a man with tremendous curiosities about the world that stood at a distance from me. His accounts of travels and the various incidents were not only helping me to understand what a *dervishes* life meant, but was also making a colossal impact on my mind.

He signalled me to follow him; we reached a place where three young men were waiting for him. The three men and I sat beside him; they seemed to be awaiting his presence for a long time. Without interrogating him, they likened themselves to listen to what he had to say.

"I do not remember much about my parents but since the time I know of myself, I have been following a path of *Tasawwuf*, purifying my heart and moving closer to god; keeping myself free from vengeance, hatred, jealousy and greed." He glanced at us through his graceful eyes for a moment and continued.

"My mother passed away when I was six and then I lived with my father, who knew a special science—he had learnt it from a Sufi many years ago. People approached him to understand the future of their relationships with each other, to seek cure for the sick and even to understand if they would obtain triumph in their ventures. As time passed, he got entangled in the affairs of the people who approached him, sometimes he would travel with them to their homes or sometimes to different places to fulfil the requests made by them."

I could sense him narrating all this in a rather dejected manner.

"He insisted that I learn this science from him. It was not money that he looked for; a mere feeling of their sincere thankfulness was enough, but as the years rolled, he felt that he possessed powers to cure people or cause harm or even do some black magic. He was overwhelmed by the idea that people started considering him second to god, and instead of praying to god they preferred seeking help from him."

"One day, there came a group of four men at our door. They looked like they belonged to a Sufi cult from Asmara. They shared their thoughts with him. While I was busy preparing a medicine that my father had asked me to, they finished with their conversation and extended blessings to both of us with a suggestion that he should be careful and should not make a display of his spiritual powers to the world, but keep it to him. They indicated that sometimes the acquired knowledge

Benazir Patil

caused more harm than good. But my father did not feel uneasy, instead he reacted that these so-called men of god are jealous of the powers that god had conferred on him. I was but a child and could not identify much with what was happening."

"A few days later, one morning, lying in his bed, he called me and said that perhaps he is soon going to die. He started palpitating and jabbering: "The two angels, Munkar and Nakir, are questioning me, 'who is your lord?' I am telling them the truth, but they are not believing me. Please help me convince them, my son."

"He took my hand in his, drew me closer to him and said, 'I have committed an unforgivable sin; I took pride in doing prophecy and forgot that destinies were designed by god and not by us. I seek god's mercy on me that my repentance be paid.""

Shah baba continued "His death revealed a lot, and then onwards I drifted into the valley of quest and stumbled upon several difficulties and trials." He took a long pause as he said this.

"What was this valley of quest?" I could not resist myself

"It is a valley with different streams. Streams of love, which has nothing to do with reason; streams of space which reveals the impermanence of knowledge; streams of detachment that reveal that no desire to possess or a wish to discover anything beyond our present can challenge the will of god. It was this detached will that overwhelmed me."

I was hearing attentively.

I was astonished completely by the conversation he was having with us. He had an inherent disposition of getting lost in his own thoughts.

I had questions hidden in every corner of my mind, it was only when I would see and hear something the questions triggered and came to the fore. And no sooner I got involved into gauging why things were the way they were. However, I kept coming back to one solitary question, over and over again, why was I here in this universe?

I went home and opened the *Ketaab-e-Hayaat*, Page 115 read:

I, wisdom, dwell together with prudence; I possess knowledge and discretion. To fear the LORD is to hate evil; I hate pride and arrogance, evil behavior and perverse speech. Counsel and sound judgment are mine; I have understanding and power.

Prudence: People with prudence have self-restraint, they have the ability to keep oneself from being misled.

Jesus instructed his disciples to be "wise as serpents and harmless as doves". He asked us to be prudent to discriminate between truth and error.

Prudence is the first pillar of wisdom.

Knowledge and discretion: Part of wisdom involves knowing how to avoid danger.

The second pillar of wisdom is to possess knowledge of Sagacious things. Knowing what is going on about you so that you can wisely plan for the future and avoid any potential dangers or evils.

Fear of God: To fear the LORD is to hate evil; our lives are committed to God's purpose. It entails serving, worshipping, obeying and loving him. It also means turning from evil and hating evil.

To fear the Lord, is the third pillar of wisdom.

Counsel: Counsel means to give wise guidance. It also means to listen to counsel. Even the wisest and godliest have made errors in discerning things. We must seek counsel instead. And we can do this by weighing up a matter in the presence of God through prayer and also through inviting counsel from other experienced believers.

Counseling and listening to the counsels is the fourth pillar of wisdom.

Sound Wisdom: Sound wisdom means behaving each day with righteousness, justice and equity, these three great themes being the basis of your behaviour.

This is the fifth pillar of wisdom

Understanding: To understand we must discern wisely between good and evil.

Understanding is the sixth great pillar of wisdom.

Power: The man with godly wisdom is truly strong and fortified. He or she is truly fortified against the evils of this world and is a true servant of God.

Power is the seventh pillar of wisdom.

18

He looked at me distantly as if he was not surprised at all with my presence. There seemed to be a vague understanding between the two of us as if we knew each other for long.

"Looks like I have met you before" I told him with a bit of hesitation.

"It may be true if you are feeling so." He said

"You don't seem to be sure if you have met me ever?" I asked.

"Not really! In fact, to me every person I meet is the one with whom I have had some connection in the past either in this life or before I came into this world". He said

"That's strange; does that mean all of us are living several lives?" I asked

"I am not sure about others but my own vibrations do spell out that this is not my first coming to the universe". He said

"And how do you determine that?" I asked

"It is inexplicable," he said.

"Why?"

"Because I am unable to tell you how my mind analyses my own existence. Perhaps there could be a thing about you that you may also find difficult to tell me about the way you analyze all the happenings in your life," he responded.

That was how Shosyos and I had first met, seamlessly.

He was almost true when he said that to me. I had never explained much about the happenings in my life, had I made an attempt I probably would not have been able to. Strangely a stranger had revealed this truth to me.

While leaving from Yazd I was determined that I will continue to have onward journey without many breaks to Fatehpur. But something about Balkh had held me back. Perhaps Shosyos was the important of all the things.

Shosyos had never been to school; he could neither read nor write. As days passed by, his talks started becoming more interesting to me, his narration of stories said as if he had lived there over a few centuries. Neither a hermit, nor a businessman, he worked as a farmer. He religiously looked after his ancestral land that the legacy had bestowed on him. My first impression of him as someone idle had not just changed drastically but was also causing an enormous transformation in my own intellect. Witnessing his brilliant oratory was a charm. He had his own ways of telling me about the things he had heard of from no-where.

"You bring me a riddle, a mystery," I told him.

"You are in that phase of life when your inquisitiveness is as unmanageable as it was in your infancy and the environs around you are merrily adding more curiosity to it," he said.

"How could I not be curious after I have befriended you? Tell me more."

"About what, my friend? You would have met with philosophers, poets, artists and warriors; I am none of them. Those are the great men who bring us to understand the truths of life, tell me what you want to understand from me?" he asked.

"What is the definition of a great man according to you?" I asked him.

"One whose life proves him to have been recognized, if not called, by God," he responded.

Everywhere I moved around with him, he passionately recited to me the rhymes about the land of Rumi and Rabiah, and deepened my understanding of the glorious Sufi worldview.

"*Zarthosht*'s first preaching and his inevitable end came on this very land you have your feet on to, the same land that has swept my imaginations immensely". He told me with delight.

His narrations about the birth and the death of the mystifying prophet made me feel as if *Zarthosht* would just walk in amongst the two of us to initiate some new lessons. At times, I smiled to myself with a thought that he almost seemed to me like Daniyaal. Just the way I discussed my dreams with Daniyaal, I was tempted to tell him one of the dreams that I had seen that morning, it was partially interesting because of the feeling that I had probably dreamt of this a few times before. I tried to recall, but could not remember anything at all.

"Do you dream?" I asked

"Sometimes in sleep, yes, but many times when I am just walking around" said Shosyos with a smile

"What do you see?" I asked

"When I am walking around some places, I feel as if I have been there before, I can see that I had lived in that house and I sometimes also get to see and feel what I was doing then"

"But this is just your imagination, how do you call this a dream?" I asked

"This may not be a reality and it may not be happening at that moment, but I know that this has happened in the past or may happen in future someday, the pictures remain alive in my mind, so I feel this is also a dream"

Perhaps Shosyos was right in what he was saying, I had been through this feeling too, but never figured out what it meant.

"Why are you asking all this Khuda?"

"I dreamt of something last night and perhaps have dreamt the same thing few times before, wondered if you will be able to understand anything about it."

"Why not, let me hear and understand if it means anything," he said

"I saw that I was preaching to a woman, that she should pray. When she asked me how she should be doing that, I told her to ask her seven body parts about it. As she was to question me further about what I meant by that, I realized that I had woken up and there was nobody around me, I recalled and could not remember anything about the woman," I told him.

"This is very simple to understand," he smiled and said.

"How?" I asked.

"Perhaps you did not ponder over the idea of the seven body parts. It is all about prostration; you prostrate on your feet, knees, hands and face, so that makes it to seven parts of your body. By saying this perhaps you meant that she should prostrate and thank the almighty," he said.

I was startled by his instant interpretation.

Shosyos had taught me more about the clue in my dreams. I kept silent for some time and asked: "You said yesterday that you have much more to say about this land than just about *Zarthosht* and Rumi."

"Did I say that?"

"Yes, you did, I don't know if it was about some person or a place in Balkh," I said.

"Actually, I was thinking about your dream. It reminded me of the seven-line prayer. It is a prayer that is recited by people in the land called Tibet, where they worship the 'lotus born'."

"It was perhaps not about the seven-line prayer, you wanted to say more about the historical eons of this township," I interrupted him.

"Yes, this very prayer, people reiterate this with in-depth conviction and piety. The seven-line prayer is a call to Lord Padmasambhava. When they call him, he comes to their rescue like a mother who cannot resist the call of her child. Many centuries ago when the exalted Buddha was breathing his last, he shared with his disciples the principles of inevitability of death and his passing into *Nirvana*. He asked them to await the birth of the Lotus-born in the lake of Dhanakosha in Uddiyana after twelve hundred years," said Shosyos with a pause.

I sat completely perplexed trying to figure out what Shosyos was talking about. I was absolutely in oblivion of Lord Padmasambhava, but had a little knowledge of the Buddha that I had received from Zeba.

"The lake of Dhanakosha is located here, Balkh was known as Uddiyana once. The Buddha also declared that Lord Padmasambhava would be wiser, more powerful than him and will spread the message of the secret mantra."

My eyes were slowly filled with hunger and curiosity to know more.

"There ruled a king in this land, who was blind, but very wealthy. One day when his only son passed away, the kingdom was faced with a massive adversity and famine. It is said that the king travelled to the depth of the sea to procure the wish-fulfilling gem. The gem healed him of his blindness and his eyes spotted an eight-year-old child sitting in a lotus flower in Lake Dhanakosha. The king adopted this child and the kingdom regained its glory. This child was Lord Padmasambhava, the second Buddha. His spiritual reality transcended time and space and he is worshipped today in many parts of the world," Shosyos concluded

"So much you know about this part of the world!" I exclaimed

"It is not about knowledge; it is my love for exploring the antiquity, to understand how our ancestors lived and what they perceived about their lives," he said.

"Indeed, just the way this land has nourished the divinity of Sufis and the doctrines of the Paracletes such as the *Zarthosht* and Lotus Born, every corner of the world must have had souls who revealed the beauty of life" I said.

"Khuda, I do not think it is over and gone. It is a cycle: from time to time the world witnesses the emergence of these holy souls who rejuvenate the thoughts and teachings of the past."

That evening I wanted to reflect more on what Shosyos had told me; I pulled out the *Ketaab-e-Hayaat* and opened Page 43, it read:

The Seven Principles of Huna

In the Huna tradition there are 7 basic principles that govern life and the creation of existence. The 7 fundamental principles of Huna are:

IKE: Our ideas create our reality. The world is what we think we are. The reality of our experience comes from within.

KALA: There are no limits in this universe except those created in our own mind. The only thing stopping us from reaching our full potential, our goals and dreams is our mind.

MAKIA: Energy flows where attention goes. Wherever there is a flow of energy and attention, events are created.

MANAWA: Now is the moment of power. There is no power in the past and there is no power in the future.

ALOHA: To love is to be happy with. Love is happiness.

MANA: All power comes from within. The power to create flows through you. This flow of energy is moulded by what manifest in your life as your creations.

PONO: Effectiveness is the measure of truth. There is no one truth, method or technique to be happy. There are many, many ways to achieve happiness. This is Pono. There is always another way to do anything.

The Huna shamans believe in our life as being another form of a dream.

19

Balkh was supposed to be a stopover; however I had extended my stay. I continued to stay with Shosyos for a few days, but soon I was to exhaust the little money I had on me. I realized I needed to search for some work. I decided to look for work the next morning; I reached the market and found the hustle bustle of traders; I tried to talk to some of them, but people were too busy.

I approached an old man who was quietly managing the work while he sat in his shop.

"What do you want," he asked me.

"I am looking for some work; I need to earn a living."

"Are you from Balkh?"

"No, I have come from Yazd."

"Are you married?" he asked me. I was a little startled by his question.

"No."

"Then would you like to work in one of my Caravanserais?"

"What will I need to do?" I asked him.

"You will soon learn about it, do not worry."

"How soon can I start and what will you pay me?"

"Come afresh tomorrow morning and start. There is a group of people from Bukhara who will need help; I will tell you about your wages then."

I came back to the fields and looked for Shosyos. I found him deeply engaged in some kind of meditation. Not wanting to disturb him, I sat next to him with my eyes closed. The beauty of nature around was bountiful, but the serene solitude had engulfed my heart; in just a few moments I entered a completely different world. Brilliance was spreading around me, peace was flowing with the winds, I felt the soft caress of the breeze on my body. Without realizing anything I prostrated to Mother Earth, blissfully receiving her vibrations. As I stood up, I found Shosyos gazing at me.

"There is a unique radiance in your eyes at this moment," he said.

"Is it something unusual?" I asked him.

"Yes, surely, I have been watching you for the last few weeks, but have not seen this radiance before, it looks like you have reached the stage of *Piti*," he said.

"What is that?" I asked.

"Words will not be able to explain to you what I am trying to say, you are in a different state of consciousness, it is a sense of happiness that comes from within, if you do not know what it means, do not worry, nature will bestow its knowledge on you when it is required for you to understand," he said.

"I can understand what you mean; perhaps happiness cannot resist itself when you listen to the delightful songs of Mother Earth" I said.

"I agree, the winds, the mountains, the flowers, the meadows, all are reflecting her happiness," he said.

"There are times when I have heard her cry too, times when she asked me to stay back and spread some peace, times when she told me to move ahead to places where people are waiting for me. Rarely has she told me to just be there and enjoy her serenity," I said.

"I envy you, you are a lucky child of hers; miserable are those who are unable to hear her and talk to her, I am still learning the process of reaching her. I find that all our life is a mere struggle, half of it is spent in struggling to reach wealth and glory and the other half not letting it go," he paused for a moment and continued.

"But you are different my friend, you are well versed with the secrets of grief and happiness, neither losses can cause you misery, nor can treasures soar you high, you can cure people of their worldly maladies," he said.

Darkness was setting in; the moon above us was preparing itself to shine in full beam. I listened to his words and knew that he was gradually transcending from his mortal self to a divine self. The next morning I woke him up with the first ray of the sun.

"Come, the eyes of the sun are waiting to see you, it is time that you listened to Mother Earth." The spirit in him woke up as I said that to him; he followed me as if I was extending some heavenly knowledge to him.

"Let us prostrate to Mother Earth and quietly listen to her feelings." Without any questions, he obeyed and knelt to prostrate. He stood up after few minutes and wept bitterly, as if something had shaken him. After a few moments of silence, he spoke.

"Have you the knowledge of what the Buddha said about enlightenment?" he asked.

"Enlightenment! I had heard of it from Shah Baba once, what is that?"

"It means to get awakened to your reality, your very existence."

"Am I not awake now?"

"That is what I told you, you have started moving towards it."

"Towards what?"

"The facets or the phases of being awakened; there are seven facets that one interacts with and you have already started connecting with those."

"I do not understand what you are saying."

"Slowly you will."

"The first facet is *sati*, where you can distinguish between the beauty and the ugliness of your deeds; the second, *dhamma vicaya* is a facet of keen investigation, seeing things as they really are. The whole universe is constantly changing, not remaining the same for two consecutive moments. The third is *viriya*, energy, where you have to make efforts and work out your own deliverance. And the fourth is *piti*, the facet of joy and happiness that comes from within."

I was suddenly reminded that he had mentioned this to me the other day.

"Yes, it is the same phase I was referring to, I can see the happiness, the one that emerges from the depth of your heart, you have to walk further to the other three states, to get awakened."

"What are the other three?"

"You will know it, gradually, your mindfulness will grow."

Every word of his was so perfectly clear, so proven.

Shosyos, barely 16 years old, gave me the message of the world's symmetry, that everything that transpires is linked, our meeting too was bound by some law of the universe; our connectivity already existed, through thoughts, through meditation, through realizations and through enlightenment.

My contemplative mind reached for the *Ketaab-e-Hayaat*: "would it have something on enlightenment?" I thought.

I opened Page 142, it read:

> *Seven subtle bodies exist within this one body of ours. Like layers of an onion*
>
> *Three physical plane bodies on lower side and three spiritual plane bodies on higher side.*
>
> *The astral body is the bridge between the lower and higher bodies. All of these possess energies, the energies from the higher planes pass through the "fire of the heart" to reach and be of full use by the lower bodies.*
>
> *First Layer is the physical body.*
>
> *Second Layer is the emotional body, associated with our feelings.*

Third Layer is the mental body that holds our thoughts.

Fourth Layer is the astral body, the bridge to the spiritual plane!

The Fifth Layer is the etheric body.

The Sixth Layer is the spiritual body, our consciousness.

The Seventh Layer is the Causal Body, the one that pulsates and vibrates and brings about our oneness with god.

I pondered if the seven states of enlightenment were connected to these seven subtle bodies that existed within one body. More than often, the words from the *Ketaab-e-Hayaat* pushed me into a whirlwind of thoughts, sometimes so deep that I found it difficult to come out. But at the same time, it had carried me into this blissful phenomenon called walking with the humanity; I had had lingering thoughts of being the person I wanted to be. As my thoughts unfolded, questions about how the whole humanity moved, what it desired, and how it aspired continued to erupt in my mind frequently.

It was ironical that I was aspiring to live a life without aspirations.

Was it possible to exist like a myth, and live beyond occasions, instances and moments? I was aspiring to live in the timeless world. As my thoughts started to turn into concepts in my mind, the clarity of a direction in life dawned onto me. Despite being at ease with myself, I had been working on freeing others from the burden of concerns they had for me; this was a task which I decided to take upon myself and the very mission of doing so opened the gates to a life filled with freedom and joy. From that moment onwards,

I knew no dilemmas, no fears and no search for the spirit; I needed no shields or security.

However, I was not spared of the usual lessons: I was asked to believe life comprised of failures and triumphs coming in turns; how good or bad we performed purely determined our rewards or punishments, manifesting our presence in either heaven or hell. I had no heart to condemn this whatsoever, but something inside me assured that there was much more to human existence than just the final path to either of the two abodes.

My sustained analysis of all the reading I did convinced me that every religion evolved with some rational understanding. It may have been just perceptions, at times, of a few individuals struggling to pave a path to create goodness and destroy depravity. The struggle remained inconclusive. Then there came interpreters who tried to provide with meanings to all those who were considered to be ordinary, ordinary like me perhaps. However, things became difficult for the ordinaries that were left lurching between the messages the religions gave and the influences that message interpreters fostered.

Zeba had taught me that I should be what I wanted to be and do what I wanted to do.

I had asked her: "so you mean only I should decide how to live my life, you mean nobody else will bother and tell me what I should be doing?"

"It is not that nobody will say anything to you or suggest, there will be thousands around you, who would tell you what to do and what not to do; there will be people who will tell you about wrongs and rights, sins and virtues; there will be people who will trouble you and who will make you happy; there will be people who will commend you and some who will disapprove of you; many who will confuse you and many who will want to take charge of your life. But, you are not to be living by all of these people's say, you will have to be living by what the person in you says, and what your conscience will guide you to do," she responded.

And I questioned her again: "and what if my heart and mind would ask me to do wrong things and not the right ones, how will I come to know of them?"

"God has made you in his own image, so the one who created you, lives in with you there inside your heart, so listen to the voice that comes from there, that will always ask you to do the right things."

"And what else will God ask me to do from inside, Zeba."

"He will guide you to love others, be good to them, to never cheat anyone and to be honest in every moment, be it of despair or happiness."

I could never understand what Zeba meant by 'God' residing inside me, because for me I believed that it was Zeba who had created me and so if there was anyone who lived inside me, it was Zeba, and so all my questions were meant for her and all the answers were to come from her alone. I continued to live by this conviction, so much so, that I would knock my heart and ask her, "Zeba, tell me what should I do?" and I would hear her voice as my answer.

Gradually, as I grew up, I realized that Zeba's answers differed from the world I lived in. The humanity around me had verily been taught to eat, to think, to love and to sleep as per the established plan. Everything was to happen as per the defined rules, with complete cognition and for obvious results. Nobody knew if this meant leading a perfect or imperfect life. But, it gave me clear indications of the need to find myself even if I got lost into something. Even if I felt like a stranger, I had to become familiar; even if I was a dreamer I had to align myself with the realities, and even if I longed to live in the forests I had to acclimatize with the hustle-bustle of the crowds.

Benazir Patil

20

Like a monk I had moved from one cave to another. Having got carried away by its magnificence, I quite imagined the days when the real monks had lived there.

A vision appeared before my eyes, as though something hidden was getting revealed. I was travelling back in time towards nothingness. I had housed myself in the ruins of Bamiyan. But the ruins were haunting me to a glorious and spiritual sensation. I had exceptionally experienced such a magnetic attraction flowing into me from all seven directions of the universe. I humbled myself and prostrated on the ground. I could hear the waves of the sea and the storms of the mountains and the chanting of the monks merging with the natural music of nature. The fluttering of the birds and the hustle bustle of the animals pictured a serene soul seated amongst them. My eyes brightened with the site of the tranquil smile of the Buddha. It was not a strange experience. I felt as if my whole being was linking my present to a distinct but spiritual past and was taking me to the echoes of emotional and melodious enlightenment. Something around woke me up. It was the misery and shackles of the ruins once again. I realized there was a spirit around me whose breath was scattering god-like warmth. The world was full of temples and edifices built in the names of heavenly fathers and mothers. They were glorified till the times the chosen disciples were able to live comfortably around those. Human acts of overpowering each other had often silenced this set of disciples and had gradually casted a shadow of darkness leading the once-upon-a-time spiritual valleys to turn into ruins like these. Oft times I felt the spirit of the

Buddha talking to me of *nirvana*, of the human misery, of the knowledge and ignorance, of the perishing bodies and their emptiness.

Sitting in the city of the dead, I had entered the city of life. I pondered over the human struggle to create wealth, customs, laws, and ways of worshipping. I pondered verily of the narrowness of human mind to create temples outside the soul rather than creating inside them, deserting the outside ones as per convenience and comfort. The thought of god creating man in his own image has been losing its essence continuously as mankind is growing, occurred to me once again. Men search for spirituality in the environs and do not seek the one they have been blessed with inside of them. It was natural for man to search for the almighty somewhere outside; it is rare that he sees Him at home in fathers and mothers, in the acts of kindness, and the solitude within.

As evening approached, I walked along the streets in the market looking for an inn. The market looked promising enough for some meaningful employment. My thoughts kept retreating to the caves; I had felt lost in the tall, blank, mud-rendered walls. Shosyos had told me about the three Buddhist monks who had travelled to Gandhara to spread the message of the Buddha. The city had earned its holiness then.

Deeply engrossed in my thoughts, I found myself standing in front of a mansion; it did not look like an inn but the night was dark enough and I had to find some shelter for myself. Just as I was about to knock the door, I heard footsteps behind me. A tall middle-aged man stood behind as I turned around to look. A questioning look on his face was too obvious. I tried telling him in broken Dari that I was looking for a place to stay for the night. It was quite unusual a demand for him, he confirmed if I was new to the town. I did not look like a thief I thought, but that is what every thief would be thinking. Without intending to convince him of my innocent motive, I decided to move ahead. To my surprise, he gestured me to come inside and asked me to unburden my sack on the side. Having gauged that I was tired after a long day he offered me some water.

Before I could question him about anything, he spelt out his name and enquired mine. His name was Mir Raza; he was staying there with his ailing father. I could see no other soul residing in that large mansion which was no less than a palace. Keen to know about my whereabouts and my purpose to visit Bamiyan, he asked me a few questions, which I answered to his satisfaction. After showing me the room adjacent to the main door, he signalled me that I could sleep there peacefully.

The next morning, he was up and ready before I could. He offered me breakfast and enquired about my journey ahead.

"It looks like I will try and find some work for myself and stay here for some time," I told him.

With no great surprise he responded, "Do you know anyone here?"

It was indeed commendable that he was making every effort to bring some Persian into his language for the sake of my understanding.

"No, I am alien to this place, but I will try and find something to sustain myself very soon," I said.

He seemed to be startled at my confidence and wondered if I had lost my family in some epidemic and for some obvious reasons had turned into a nomad.

"Work is fine, you may get it, but you will also have to look for a place to stay." He added with a deep thought.

"I can help you in getting some work, I have my business of spices, and you could assist me in that, but there is something more important that I am looking for."

"What is that?" the expressions on my face revealed so many words.

"I am the only child of my parents. After my mother passed away, I have been looking after my father; now he is very ill and bed-ridden, I need to take care of him, I try and stay home as often as possible, but realize that my business is suffering because of this and I am afraid that I will soon have to bear some losses. I have been looking for a trusted caretaker for him."

He stopped at that; I understood what he was going through and also his gesture of offering me this job.

"If you are even half-willing to help me, I shall introduce you to my father Shamsher Raza, and you could then decide," he said.

I was a stranger to him, but he looked at me as a trusted caretaker. I wasn't surprised; I often found people confiding in me their most untellable secrets, I had rarely met someone who questioned my integrity.

The next day he took me around the house. He seemed to be a learned man—he had a library full of books written in Arabic, Pashtu, Persian and even local scripts that looked similar to Persian but when I tried to understand the titles of some of those books, I could not understand much. I was fascinated to see his collection.

Shamsher had already crossed the eighty-first year of his life: his face had wrinkles carved out of sweat and toil; his gestures were kind and a fresh mind like his looked emphatic.

His beard, streaked with white, added more lustre to his face.

Mir Raza introduced me to him and my eyes met with his, he almost blinked at me like a small child, as if I was a long lost old friend.

"I am not ill, just bedridden, am not able to move around, I should be served by others is god's wish for me," he explained, without waiting for my questions.

"So I am enjoying my time, many of my friends have already left the world, there are few visitors for me now."

He looked at me and asked Mir Raza in a very subtle manner if I was his friend or a business acquaintance.

"Khudabakhsh is new to the town. He has been travelling from Hamadan and has to go to some place in Hindustan, and on his way he decided to spend some time in Bamiyan. Yesterday he was looking for a place to stay for some days and I offered him that he can stay with us," said Mir Raza.

"That is wonderful, so Khudabakhsh, are you on some business trip, do you intend to sell something?" Shamsher asked me.

Most of the times I had replied to people straight away that I was a wanderer and that I was not in search of any purpose, but for the past few months, sometimes I did think that I was searching for a purpose. I thought for a moment about the authenticity and transparency of my mind and said, "I do not have any specific goal in life, but I definitely know that I have a purpose to be fulfilled and my heart says that I am on that path towards my purpose. My travel has nothing to do with any business; in fact, I keep taking up odd jobs in every place where I stop for some time to earn some livelihood and refrain from being dependent on anyone."

"Oh what a life, I wish I could live like you," he said.

"All of us are wanderers in our hearts, Khudabakhsh, and we want to go places and experience the world, but the way our lives are designed, that we live each day with some planning—sometimes it feels good to know and understand our plans—but gradually we realize that our plans become more dominant in our lives than our hearts, we listen more to the plans than the latter. There comes a time when we do realize what we are doing, but then it is difficult to undo many things that we have already worked out based on our plans," he added.

"Have you been unhappy about the way you have lived your life?" I asked him

"No, it is not about happiness or unhappiness, contentment or discontentment; it is all about the searching and seeking that we do since the time we gain consciousness," he responded.

"There was a man who lived in my village many years ago. He had heard someone say: "if you try hard, you can even find god," so he decided to find god and so all his life spent seeking and searching god. He would try out many things, sometimes he would observe the stars and try to find god there, sometimes he would talk to human beings and look into their eyes and say that perhaps god resided in them, sometimes he would just feed his naïve sheep and feel good about it—he had so many probabilities to share about god's residence that people thought he had gone mad. One day, someone told him that behind a hill there was a cave and god lived in it. He decided to climb the hill and walk down to the cave. He even reached the cave, but as he was about to enter, he stopped and thought to himself, that if he finally found god inside, what would he do for the rest of his life? His search would be over and there would be no purpose left for his existence anymore. He turned around and walked back to his village; he had started enjoying the act of searching for god that had become the very cause of his existence; he wanted to enjoy that expedition of search."

I was listening with great interest.

"So, we all live by plans and goals, but many times when these goals are achieved, we do not know what to do next, then we look for newer goals and not always do we find them. Sometimes, the efforts of working towards a goal are much more reaping and fulfilling than the goal itself, but humans do not understand this; they like to measure achievements in numbers and that is where they lose the ability to experience the truth."

Shamsher was right in what he was sharing with me; I immediately grasped the fatal battle he must have been through to earn enough to live in a palatial mansion he was residing in and perhaps by living in that very mansion he was realizing what was so great about being there.

After some discussions the three of us had a good feasty lunch prepared by the cook who came every morning. I decided to stay back and serve as a caretaker of Shamsher.

I started looking after Shamsher's needs and thanked god for his company. We discussed so much about the books, and he had started teaching me a new language called Urdu, which was in many ways similar to Persian. He even shared a lot of poetry with me and had so much to explain about each line.

One morning when I was approaching Shamsher's room, I happened to see a man with three heads. It seemed to me as if there was someone sitting there who had three heads attached to his neck. I was startled! It reminded me of my dream and its message. I rushed closer to see who the man was; I realized that it was Shamsher himself who was sitting on the bed with his two legs half folded on the sides, hunched and his head popping up from in between; his two knees seemed to me like two additional heads. As I continued to think of what I perceived from far and what it actually meant, I was reminded of Daniyaal's words that I will be able to unfold the meaning of my dreams myself. The man with three heads was not literal; it was a man of wisdom as Shamsher.

I saw Shamsher lost in some deep thoughts, but the moment he saw me he smiled and asked me what the matter was. He had this knack of guessing very easily if I was engrossed in some thoughts.

"Nothing much," I said.

I sat still for some time; I went out, made some tea for both of us and returned with new thoughts brewing up in my mind.

I looked at him and asked, "what did you aspire to become in your childhood?"

"I wanted to become a human," he said.

A logician by heart, he had a lot to share about his experiences.

"Why do you say human, we are all humans by birth, what is there in it if you aspire to become human?" I asked him.

Benazir Patil

"The characteristics of a human are actually the qualities and traits that god possesses and these are merely reflected in human nature when you observe human beings closely. God has immeasurable qualities and you read about it in scriptures coming down to us from antiquity; you find a vivid description of it in almost every holy book; ninety-nine of these are mentioned in the holy Quran also," he said.

"And how do you express this?" I asked him.

"Every human that comes to the world is born in the image of god, therefore in small children we often witness godly ways. It is when these children grow up to be an adult they get centred around their ego, so much so that they sometimes deny and defy the existence of a spiritual power. Their life gets carried away by illusions and imaginations and these very illusions keep them away from their spiritual journey," he responded.

"What are these illusions?" I asked him

"There lived a great saint in Hindustan, whose thoughts emphasized only one thing: everything that exists in the world is deceptive and misleading—he called this deception *maya* an illusion. Everything in this world is assumed by us as the reality which may or may not be, that we exist and the whole world exists with us, that we are someone and we possess this world, all these could be just assumptions. His message was simple: just as the physical world exists, the celestial world also exists, and so do time and space, and we do not know from where this time came or how this space was created, but we still try to possess time and space, we still try our best to conquer these without realizing our inability to do so," he concluded.

He was talking of the ultimate reality, beyond time and space.

21

I looked at the sunlit tranquillity around me. It had been long I had not opened the *Ketaab-e-Hayaat,* Shamsher's talks had a magical power; everytime I heard him, it made me feel like referring to a leaf from my book. I wondered if he also had a book like mine or he possessed it in a different form as Daniyaal had explained to me.

I opened the chest where I kept all my things I required for daily chores. The book lay wrapped in fine yellow satin Shosyos had given me when we parted. I un-wrapped it, opened Page 16, it read:

God's Messenger says:

> *God will shade seven groups of people under His shade on the Day when there will be no shade except His:*

>> *The just ruler;*

>> *Young people who have grown up in worship of God;*

>> *Those who are greatly attached to mosques;*

>> *Two persons who love each other for God's sake, meet and then leave each other because of this love;*

>> *Men who refuse the invitations of beautiful women of rank, saying "I fear God";*

Those who spend in the way of God so secretly that when they give charity to the one on his left, the one on the right does not see it;

And those whose eyes fill with tears when they mention God in seclusion

Those who wish for His shade must strive for being at-least one of the above.

I read it thrice, the fourth one struck my mind. Suddenly, a fragrant serenity possessed my heart. I wondered if I were also to meet someone. I blushed at my abrupt realization of my youthfulness.

Just then I heard Shamsher calling for me, I turned to attend to him.

"Why don't you learn the trade from Mir Raza and earn some more money for your onward journey?" he asked me with no hesitation.

"Learning the trade, I do not intend to earn anything beyond my meagre needs, and I do not even want to possess anything."

"Yes, but the experience that you do not want to possess anything has no meaning when you really do not possess anything today," he paused and continued.

"It is only when you taste life's desires; you go through the test of forsaking overindulgence. I have worked hard and earned a fortune for myself, it took me long to give up and rehabilitate myself to the simplicity of god's design."

Business had never been my cup of tea but helping Mir Raza in his business and reducing some of his burden was worthwhile. Shamsher encouraged me enough to get into it. Mir Raza too, felt more than happy that I would assist him in his business.

Initially everything seemed complicated, but soon I learnt the art of talking to the traders, understood how the shipments were done for the spices and also learned to keep the accounts.

Soon, I started balancing my time between Shamsher and business, my life was no more carefree as earlier and I had to plan my day while I lay in bed the previous night; there were traders and negotiations for getting the right returns, there was writing of new accounts and settling of the old ones. There was money borrowed and money lent.

I soon learned to write down important correspondence to the far off traders who came once in a while to pick up the materials. Mir Raza trusted me the most, I thought, and shared the minutest details of the business.

"This man," Mir Raza once expressed to his friend, "is no great businessman, for the first time he is dealing with accounts and trading, but there is something about him, business has prospered three times since the time he has joined me."

"I think he has the understanding of the traders, if not the trade," replied his friend.

My interest in trade was gradually increasing, not for the richness of the monies, but for the interesting people I met with: there were traders from Hindustan too and I was always curious to find if I could someone from Fathepur.

Benazir Patil

I was building Mir Raza's business with utmost affection; he also did pass on a lot of shares from his profits to me, which I many times refused but had to take it at times when he refused to give up.

And there came a time when the business incurred huge losses; it had to do with many things: the bad monsoons, the wars that had restricted travel for the traders to come to Bamiyan to fetch the spices.

But this was not the end; I realized I needed to pour more love into my work, and I worked harder than before to bring back the business on track. Shamsher, nevertheless, was a guiding force who always told me, "The best form of gain is the one that comes through the work with your own hands and through every legitimate sale."

We shall never understand one another until we reduce the language to seven words

Kahlil Gibran

22

I looked in the mirror and tried to recall who I was.

Where was I lost? Had my life been a long spell or had it just begun? Gazing at my own image had not helped; my reflection displayed that I was not a child anymore but a grown up man. It seemed that I had lived for many years, reminiscences, however, were none. I was doing a great favour to myself by leading this clueless time married with complete patience. Though I lacked the insistence to know myself, the silence around me was loudly asking me to utter something. Having woken up from my sleep, both inflexible and tired, I tried hard to lift myself up from bed; I could not, my neck had given up too, and it refused to support my head. The feeling was confusing. Unsure of my existence and the place where I lay, I closed my eyes, meditated for some time, opened them again and looked through the window. Nothing seemed familiar.

Outside the window stood a man; his face seemed familiar, he had come over to me thrice in the last few hours. He kindly ensured my wellness. As he noticed me looking at him, he turned around and entered the room thinking that I was up to tell him something. His eyes questioned me if I had recalled who I was. But when he probed my expressionless face, with great conviction, he babbled some words in my ears. The words however were of no consequence to me.

"*Om Tat Sat*" he uttered.

Thoughtlessness was not the state I was into. Neither was I living a life of nothingness. I had walked through the toughest moments life had demanded me to, but this was strange. Suddenly life seemed to have lost all its connections with me; my mind was drifting with the wind. It was not the mirror alone that was not revealing me my identity, the walls around me, the mud that lay on my floor, the window next to my bed, the sky that peeped in through that window, all were refusing to tell me the truth about myself. I could barely recall that I had been walking for years; neither could I recall the path I belonged to.

Matured mind is preceded by increased age, but I had no clue what my age was and whether my mind had any maturity to understand what was going around me. It felt like for centuries I had been living with this mystery of my presence in this world. Sometimes I felt that I was not just one person, I was the whole humanity. I looked lonely to myself, but I was not. After years and years of existence and constant recollections, inadvertently, I found myself at a loss of experiencing where those moments had disappeared from my mind. The new moments had perhaps replaced all the earlier memories that occupied my mind.

Being absolutely unsure of my destination I had gradually realized that I was living in this house for the last two days, in a town called Gujranwala. I wondered if I had imagined myself to have lived in that place ever, not that I had any greater imaginations and ideas about the places that I had visited in the past. There were strange vibrations that I was surrounded with, completely different from the ones I had got in all the alien lands that I was onto after I had left from Hamadan.

There lay a book beside me. I looked at it and made no attempt to open and see what it contained. My only interactions had been with the prayer-man who uttered prayers in my ears the first thing in the morning. Yet another man who came in seemed like a doctor. The prayer-man continued to serve me by bringing food and water every day without fail. Sometimes, I would be hungry and eat it but most often I did not feel like. Confined to my bed with very poor energy levels, my mind was incapable of meditating on anything. At times, I felt like walking out and seeing what lay on the other side of the window—my guts however refused to let me do that. The confidence of walking a few steps seemed to have been snatched away from me.

After a few hours a woman stepped in with another man who looked very humble. He examined me, checked the strength in my limbs, and asked me if I could get up and walk. I could barely understand what he said and I refrained from responding to his gesture. I knew that I was not doing it on purpose, but I also understood that I was being completely blank about what was going on around me. He made an attempt to talk to me and make me speak out something. Unfortunately, I did not respond. He greeted the woman and left with a kind gesture and a message that he will come again to see me. The woman continued to sit beside my bed. She looked at me and asked "Who are you my child? Do you not talk anything?" I did not know what to tell her. I tried hard to understand myself who I was. With a thought that she should not force me she patted on my shoulder, poured a smile in my entire being, and left.

Unlike the woman, the prayer-man had not made any attempt to talk to me, his eyes conversed with mine. The words whispered in my ears were one of the most satisfying experiences in my life, I thought. Having lost the world that I had lived in, it was ironical that I had started gaining an understanding of this new world that I had got exposed to. The curiosity of hearing the conversations between the woman and the prayer-man had emerged. My eyes examined everything around just like the eyes of a newborn child would. I pondered if everything around me was really new or I had just been born. There was some pain in the body; the sensations had made me realize that my body still had life in it, my brain still thinking and my intellect investigating. As the hours and days passed by I realized that I was a man who would have been born many years ago. I may have done something and lived some kind of life to have become this soul and this body. A struggle with oneself at its helm was accompanied with a fight to discover the truth about my past.

Sometimes I thought I may have been like the prayer-man earlier or like the child playing outside the window. Would I have been like that man sitting in the grocery shop selling things to people: often I pondered to retrieve the lost identities that I may have possessed before. After all the questions, I was assured only of one thing that I was nobody, a curious but uninhabited mind, a recognized but nameless being.

My struggle to know more about me was slowly transforming into an adventure to know the environs around me. This was truly a trait of a growing child, if not an inkling of an awakening soul. The pain of feeling alone was turning into a pleasure of being a lonely star that stood in the sky gazing at the world that was managing itself by several means. Conscious pain of the body was giving way to a burgeoning freshness of the mind.

In my rectangular spaced chamber, for the first few days, I just lay in my small bed. I seldom slept, the outside world was just next door, but my lack of confidence in exploring it kept me intact in my room. The waves of winds coming from the windows brought messages from the places I had been to in my past life. Deciphering those was a colossal task my mind could not deal with. A little carpet with some intricate design on my right reminded me of something, but I was not sure of what. Amidst all the disinterest I lived with, the interest in overhearing conversations between others had given birth to a new person in me. A close accessibility of my room door to their living room and the courtyard had given me this advantage and had given me a feeling of living amongst a family.

I sat watching the child on the portico. He was tearing a paper into the smallest of pieces and throwing it in the air with joy unlimited. The lens of my mind were busy comprehending something else though, the small pieces were flying in different directions as the wind took them, they had no control over their directions, they were simply led by the wind. I was not very different than those pieces of papers; it was a similar kind of wind that had reached me in the prayer-man's place.

One more face had come in that day—I was seeing him for the first time. From his conversations with the prayer-man I gathered that he was some healer, a master, or may be a learned doctor who sported the capacity of bringing me back from my lost state of mind. He seemed to have come in and seen me twice during the last few days, but I was not aware of it, perhaps he had just observed me from far. Incidentally, he was also the same man who had confirmed to the prayer-man about my state of unconsciousness when I was found lying in some place outside the town. He was the one who had ensured that I was not dumb and encouraged them to talk to me normally saying I did have the ability to talk, and that I could regain my consciousness as well as my memory very soon; however, he was unsure when.

"There are seven types of tissues in the body, each tissue has its own function; it helps to determine the identity of the self within the body. Their functions take place in seven stages, with each paving the way for the other," he said to the prayer-man's wife.

"But what were you trying to check?" she asked him.

"The *Ojas,* only that will provide him the strength to come back to what he was. I have brought these herbs for him, let me explain how you need to prepare his medicines from these." With that they both got up and left for the room outside where they talked for long about something. However, while walking outside, I overheard him saying that he was to soon teach me *pranayama*, which was one of the ways to revitalize my mind, he thought.

23

I saw her passing by my window, the rays of the moon shone on her face. I remembered the moment and wondered about the overpowering emotion I had just experienced. Then I gazed at the horizon and closed my eyes, I felt her hand on my head; it was a feeling of a king being crowned by the love of god. Every time I became conscious of her departure from the world I repeated this act of closing my eyes and looking at her. I felt like a devoted worshiper who received her blessings in those precious moments.

An enlightened being, she walked modestly in deep thoughts, her tranquil face was sans any emotion; it radiated a quiet smile that came from within. Every edge of her persona expressed peace. I wondered if I had ever before seen that calmness in my past lives. As I kept gazing at her, she wondered for a moment and moved away. Our eyes met for a jiffy, just a glance had conveyed something divine which my mind found difficult to decipher.

In the next few moments, I realized I had started to seek the essence of that one glance. I had wanted to free myself from this unidentified life I was living. Her glance had extended an unfathomable energy that was to help me overcome that sad state. Truly, there was nothing in this universe that kept me away from understanding my own self, the onus of breaking my silence lay with me alone.

Having pondered over my state of mind for some time now, one single thought caught hold of me—I knew nothing about myself; I was unaware of the world around me. Though I did not have any fears or apprehensions, as I had not fled from my soul, something in nature had made me like this. I closed my eyes to see how I could uncover the layers of dust that had gathered over my mind in the last many days. After I opened my eyes I found a quiet enthusiasm creeping into me to the very depth. For the first time I felt that I could help bring back the person that I always knew. But the task of unveiling my secrets to myself was a challenge.

I looked around, as if I had awakened from a deep sleep; the world held a meaning, though mysterious, it didn't seem unknown. I had gotten a strange energy to rise from my bed and walk out of the room. I was seeing the world for the first time. After walking out of my room—I had walked out of the mansion and had reached the veranda facing the sky—I found the way to walk ahead. The visible world was no more a deception. I decided to start a new life.

Unaware of what was happening to me, I sensed a strange desire to listen to Mother Earth, an urge to grasp the vibrations that were calling me.

Suddenly, I heard the prayer-man and his wife talking among themselves, sometimes about me, sometimes about the ways of the world. He appeared to be a professor in the city school and the woman taught Sanskrit to students that came home to learn from her. They both spoke a not-so-familiar language; I could partially comprehend what they spoke, which was indeed heartening to me. The thought that I would have spoken it sometime in my past life led me to a more positive feeling about myself.

—◦⊰⊱◦—

But something else caught my attention.

Benazir Patil

It may have been just the words or the eagerness to unearth the truth. It is so true that even the smallest stone is capable of causing an instant whirlwind in the quietest waters. For the first time I signalled myself to hear clearly the words that were flowing from one of the corners. With compressed hands and rising heartbeats, I sat up in my bed, for both the voice and the words were engraving an astonishing influence on me.

"Can I weigh your heart and measure your soul?" I heard a docile and forgiving voice interacting with the prayer-man.

"Heart has emotions and soul has vitality, but how do you measure it?" he responded to his daughter Shivani

"Yes, there lies the answer in what you feel: emotions can be felt and vitality can be gauged and that is what helps you appraise the expansion of your heart and your soul," she said.

"Have you ever seen heaven on earth?" she asked the prayer-man.

"What does it mean to you?" he asked her.

"You have come into this world and are a part of the procession that is walking towards the place you are destined to reach. During this journey you commit good and bad deeds. Every time you do a good deed, the earth delights in your presence and sends to you the winds, the stars and skies to rejoice with you and lets the peace and happiness embrace you completely. Every time you do a bad deed, the earth weeps over it, and when she weeps, you can see the peace and happiness withdrawing from you and you find it difficult to reach them. You create a heaven when you express your love for earth by doing these good deeds," she responded with a smile.

"But do not heavens reach us when we worship the supreme?" he questioned her.

"Yes, but what is this worship? Folding hands, closing eyes, and asking for the lord's mercy? We are born with all the attributes that the lord has in Him, remembering the lord is a virtue, but imitating his goodness and being good to others is the real worship. A mind full of worship and piety lives in a heaven which he has created on this very earth, and thus he does not have to struggle to imagine himself in heaven after he has left this earth," she said.

She continued to talk and the prayer-man continued to hear and respond. I sat patiently enjoying the clueless conversation, for I had no understanding of who these people were and what they were talking about.

But the conversation left me floating in the feeling of goodness. It was then I tried to recall if I had been a good or a bad man in my past life. My memory was not meant to arrive at that moment, the almighty had different plans altogether.

A child of about seventeen odd years was a teacher to her disciple thrice her age. The conversation had not ended.

"There are just so many of us in this universe, so many of us humans, animals, and so many things happening within this one life," he said.

"Yes, but each one of us is sent with a distinct plan and an embedded life." she responded.

"I sometimes feel that I am just a drop in this ocean-like universe," he said.

Benazir Patil

"Indeed, we all are, but just being a drop should not keep us away from good deeds. Every soul that thinks good of itself is like any other human being, just a drop. What matters is how we want to be: don't you feel like being an infinite drop in this infinite ocean; do you not want to be remembered infinitely by the infinity?" she said.

"We are so many of us, how is it possible that each one of us is remembered forever?" he asked.

"Your life is not about making the ordinary seem unbelievable, but of assimilating the truly unbelievable into your ordinary life; no life can be lived on an unbroken track. Perfect lives are lived with most simple rhythms and tedious challenges—overcoming these are the real treasures that humans can possess. The books of our lives are compiled by the almighty, and they remain in His treasured library, while some become his most favourite reads some remain untouched forever," she responded.

"You mean our lives are compiled by god after we have led them, but I thought they were written by Him before we were born and we just executed his writings?" he questioned her.

"Yes, you are right, our lives are designed by Him, but each of us is sent to the world with a book that guides us when we are puzzled about the ways of leading life: these are the books of lives of His most favourite children who have led their lives enchanting and spreading the goodness, they are the ones who remain in His memory forever. He is delighted when He sees us imitating His good children and liberating ourselves from all the obscurities of life; that is when He compiles our heavenly deeds, the one that seems insignificant to us, are actually recorded as the greatest in his book," she responded and continued.

The 7th Destination 155

"Have you heard the story of seven Greek sages?" she asked.

"I know about the *Sapta-rishis*, but I do not know their story," he said quizzingly.

"*Sapta-rishis*, I will, but let me first tell you about the wisdom spread by the seven Greek sages.

"Once upon a time there were seven sages in Greece who served the god Apollo. These seven spread wisdom by their words, their words initiated a lot of mystery for the scholars from across the world to unfold and understand, and these words that arrest our reflective mind are even today as influential as ever."

"What were these words?"

"These were simple but left your mind thinking, each of the sages transmitted magic into our minds."

"Magic?"

"Yes, one of them said: 'know thyself, and thou shall know the universe and the gods.' Isn't that appealing?" she said.

"Why do you think this is so appealing?"

"Because, our lives are not about days, months and years; they are about certain realizations that we need to arrive at. Our existence is nothing but a sequence of acts that are small and big: when you extend a smile to someone, it is considered a small act but that small act extends happiness, and when you toil hard for someone, it is considered a big act, because you give away your time and your physical energy for the good of that person. Both these acts stand a chance of equality when they are filled with purity," she said.

Benazir Patil

"What are these realizations?" he asked her.

"These come to us differently at different stages, in our childhood and our youth, in our happiness and our despair, and in our illness and wellness. We discover them as we grow and understand only as we experience them," she said

"And what are these?" he asked again with deeper curiosity.

"The first of these come to us in our childhood when we sense life is a mystery, impenetrable, something which we will never be able to comprehend. As we grow, the goodness and the wickedness of our fellow beings give us the second realization, of building our values. We move further into youth, and are gifted with the third truth—life does not seek your attitude but your gratitude."

I continued to hear as intently as the prayer-man did, this was no sermon, to me this was perhaps one of the realizations that she was mentioning about.

"The fourth one comes in a little late, but for some exceptional souls it is sooner than the others, acknowledging the universe for three things in our life: our mind, our body, and our soul. All through these four we do go through the miseries too, but the fifth realization dawns only when we have churned ourselves to these—never succumb to despair ushers in as wisdom."

"The sixth comes when we are walking to the conclusion; it brings in the reminders of all that was done with every passing day. It is only the seventh that is most realistic." She stopped for a moment and looked at the prayer-man.

"The seventh comes at the time of death, which neither you nor I can know; we can only perceive it, but can never know the truth about that final realization," she concluded with a smile.

I quietly enjoyed their conversation.

Absence of knowledge about me, however, withheld my conversations; I refrained from either asking anything or articulating the happenings around me. Observation was the only weapon I possessed. I did realize though as if I had been introduced to the *Ketaab-e-Hayaat* and the reality of the seven realizations. I stood there thinking about the realizations I was arriving at.

24

"Never really," I heard Shivani one morning addressing this to someone. I was listening attentively, every time I heard her I felt fresh, her thoughts were like reverberations of nourishing liveliness; her beliefs exceptionally agreeable, as if that was just what I wished to hear.

"You believe she is a good person?" her mother asked her with a tinge of anger.

"Yes, I believe so about every person! we should not force ourselves to understand so much about the people we meet; the more we think, the more we react and are inclined to judge others. Strangely, we feel hurt when we are judged by others, but we make all the effort in judging others," responded Shivani and continued after a pause.

I had gradually discovered that the evangelist-like voice belonged to a young girl named Shivani, the daughter of the prayer-man; everyone adored her. Serenity flowed through her eyes; her smile had a strange inconceivable divinity; the aura she possessed was inexplicable. A humble mortal, with wisdom of different lands, she was gifted with strengths that were little known by her contemporaries.

"Doubtlessly, we think of ourselves as gracious souls, but are often considerate only to those who have been kind to us; we do become unjust with those who have been unkind. Sometimes the intention of not wanting to be good leads to the temptation of teaching lessons to them. Revenge thus becomes inevitable. Aggression, hatred and punishment engulf our minds and we become blind to even the smallest of goodness that people have in them."

"What you say may be right my child, but what do you do when you see people doing wrong with you?" she questioned Shivani.

"Yes, we meet people who dislike us for some reasons and are unpleasant with us—they acquaint us with their vibrations and pass by. But we live with and multiply that feeling of injustice within us and reciprocate more vehemently. As we nurture hostility, we become the custodians of wrongdoings ourselves," Shivani concluded.

"It is difficult to forget the injustice done and even more difficult to forgive," her mother agitated.

"It is important that we understand this injustice, but it is essential that we hold ourselves to that soil and to those circumstances which our destinies are driving us to. A mishap or a surprise, a good or a bad, every little event occurs with a purpose and is not a matter of chance. We live for a few years and then we die, repenting and rejoicing for all that we did during our only life. When our souls are shedding our bodies, we compel ourselves to think that our existence is ending, but that is not so. It is at the fag end of our lives that we question ourselves if we lived a proper or improper life, whether we accepted or rejected the decrees set by god. We question if we understood what the world was, who we were, why the world was created and who sent us here. We see ourselves walking on a path of absolute cessation from our thoughts, our opinions, our anger, our fears and our judgments about the world; we only bond with the grief of passing away from this life to a state of death, an inevitable state we never want to get into. All our acts of aggression, power and perfidy appear worthless."

"You want me to live a life facing the wrongs that people do to me and forgive them for it rather than exposing them for what they are doing, this seems impossible." Said the mother

"No, I am not saying that. I am talking about embracing a distinct faith, a faith in which you can enthral and cling to your own goodness; a faith full of hopes, a faith that helps you discriminate between the sinner and the sin; a faith that empowers you to forgive the sinner and detest the sin. With this faith, vengeance will never be your solution; deprivation never your deed; and prejudice, never your guide, for you will live in peace, generated from within; you will not search for it elsewhere," Shivani concluded.

I sank into the depth of my own thoughts, trying to recall if vengeance and prejudice were ever the guiding forces in my life, but all in vain—I had lost the power to recall. I shook myself and wondered about the stress that I was pushing myself into as against the bliss that I was being bestowed within the spiritual environs of her thoughts.

Both the prayer-man and his wife were at a loss for words when it came to conversing with their daughter; it was perhaps easy for them to listen to a saint sitting outside their house, but difficult to deal with their own child's saintly views.

My first three weeks at the prayer-man's house seemed like an epoch; a magnificent era, where my mind was like a clean slate, with profuse absence of presumptions or fears.

The conversations I overheard set me ticking about the concepts that seemed novel to my unoccupied mind.

In those few weeks, time stood divided.

25

I wish I had some clue about that wondrous moment in which I had reached the prayer-man's house. I did not belong to his kith and kin, neither was I from this town.

Conversing with the neighbours, my eyes had started seeing the work he was doing and the bond he shared with his beloved daughter. My eyes greeted him every time he came to see me. Much affected I was every time he put his hand on my shoulder and transmitted waves of strength inside me. I had never been through an experience of having a father in so many years and had never known a man as wealthy in kindness as him. His daughter was no different; she had inherited the graciousness not from antiquity but from him and had grown into a being with noble heart with a will power beyond description.

Very soon I had overcome my loneliness and got merged with the oneness of the prayer-man's family. Despite not knowing my own identity I was living in hopeful dreams that fate had brought me to. Joy poured into my ears every time I heard her talking; I invariably got entranced and responded to their concerns with an unusual expression in my eyes.

My journey from a feeling of nothingness to solemn contentment was visible amazingly to Shivani. It was a different language that we spoke in, one of beauty and humanity, one that probably developed in timelessness. At times I felt intoxicated by the brightness of her eyes, perhaps that is why I had developed an affection so strong, one which was holding my hand and walking me to a procession of bondage from my age-old solitude. Every discourse with her gave me new insights and a new meaning to my existence. Until I reached a phase where I could memorize everything that she spoke, I could write them in the form of songs of virtue, beauty and wonder. It was like a dream of revelation which could not be measured by any yardstick of the world. The beauty lay not in her form; it lay within, in her words, expressions, and reflections. Her silence was as much music to me as were her words, even those echoed true happiness.

I remember the first time I was brought out of my room to the dinner table, with the family. All of us sat there enjoying the food but my soul was engaged elsewhere, in dreams filled with a heavenly feeling of togetherness with her.

She had got used to my silence and truly understood that speech was not the only means of conversation between two souls. Silence illuminated our souls and gave us a deeper understanding of each other. It is needless to say that everything visible on the earth was always a thought before the creation really took place.

For over a month, I had met with only the prayer-man and his wife, and had overheard a strange powerful voice every now and then. Something that day had encouraged the prayer-man to bring his daughter along with him. He had come to believe that his every effort had failed to rejuvenate memories about my past life; little did he know that I was so delighted in my present that I had stopped pressurizing myself to think about the bygone.

The conversation between the doctor and the prayer-man was of least interest and consequence to me, my eyes clashed with those of Shivani's. It was the very first time that I had seen all of her, before that moment I had heard her only conversing with others, sometimes from within my room, sometimes when I seated myself in the veranda, and sometimes when I had made severe efforts to overhear conversations with deep intent. I saw that everything within my view had tremendous brightness; the brightness of her eyes was mesmerizing yet extremely reassuring.

Her look at me abruptly made me feel as if I was a child of god with many questions deeply entrenched in me. In no time I realized that I was not alone. The prayer-man was gazing at the surprising change of expressions on my face; he was amazed to see my eyes fill with immense happiness. For the first time he saw in my eyes an urge to live. For a moment he thought I had gotten back my lost memory.

My mind tried to absorb all her attributes, sitting in my room with her hands folded, in adoration and prayer. She raised her eyes, looked at me for a moment, and examined my mind thoroughly. She expected me to utter something, but I stood speechless as usual; my mind was flooded with thoughts, but my effort to talk failed me once again. Though her presence had made me comfortable, I remained half afraid of my inability to say anything. Dressed in white, with a silk scarf draped around her neck, sans any external jewellery, she sat with a posture that reminded me of someone vaguely. However, my blank mind had nothing to tell me.

"We are fashioned by circumstances but not bound by those. We have the supremacy to exert an influence on those," she said to me with a complete faith that I had the capability to absorb everything that she said.

"If it is so, why do we struggle so much?" the prayer-man questioned her pointing at my blank expressions.

"All of us want to be fugitives sometimes, and sometimes nature converts us to one; we want to run away from the basic rationale of why we exist. Sometimes we like to blind ourselves

Benazir Patil

and do not want to see with the eyes of our understanding; sometimes we want to be poor and do not want to acknowledge all that we have that have fulfilled our needs. Therefore, sometimes we fail to see what we have and sometimes nature fails to show us what we have," she responded.

The prayer-man seemed somewhat lost. He was keen to understand my state and also knew that the words his daughter spoke were not futile: they were just a little deep for his understanding. But he did not give up. He had brought Shivani along with a purpose, he was insistent on knowing what I was going through, and why I could not express myself in speech when he could read the expressions of my mind, my eyes, and my gestures.

"Your present was your past and your future will be as your present. We all live as babies, grow up, nurture relationships, marry, have children, look after our parents, care for our loved ones, look after the sick and the dying, and play our part in the enduring play of humanity. While we do this, we also see the same humanity fighting with each other, struggling for their livelihood, robbing each other, crying with emotions, boasting about themselves, and sacrificing in humility. You see the same set of people doing this, you go away from the same people and come back to the same people, you make an effort to understand them minutely, and you find that the souls you may have loved and cared for and the same souls that you may have disliked too. There is just a single universe which is ephemeral and long-lasting at the same time. We love and despise them, and we start from one end to walk towards the other end. From whichever end we start, we reach the same kind of people wherever we go; our life continues and continues for a purpose, a purpose unknown to us," she said.

"I wonder if he understands our language?" questioned the prayer-man.

"Spoken words, he may or may not, but the expressions and emotions he definitely does. He will soon come home to the truth that his life has remained intact with him because of a purpose; he is here with us with a purpose, the loss of his memory, his inability to talk about himself also has a purpose, and so will coming back of memory have a purpose too. Many tasks of his life still remain undone; hence, he has a life ahead to finish those tasks," she said.

"You mean to say that people who die and leave this world have fulfilled their purpose?" he asked.

"Only the almighty can respond to that! Neither I nor you have the inkling of what we fulfil and do not fulfil before our end arrives. Death detaches the soul from the body, it extinguishes the feelings, emotions and actions, but within this solitary life too there are many starts and many endings. We complete infancy to start childhood, we give up childhood to enter youthfulness, and one after the other we keep concluding one stage and commencing another. With every transformation we experience death without any anguish. The truth about human life resonates with that of the universe: just as there is but one light of the sun which gets absorbed by objects galore, there is but one united soul of the whole humanity which gets distributed into several bodies, incessantly," she said.

"How do you define this boundless nature of universe as something common and united?" he asked her.

"In the seventh verse of the seventh chapter of the Gita, Lord Krishna says, there is no truth superior to me. Everything

Benazir Patil

rests upon me, as pearls are strung on a thread". She affirmed, paused for a moment, and continued to explain.

"We are an inherent fragment of this larger entity called universe, but we are not drifting in a meaningless circle; we are beings bound by unifying common factors of joys and thrill, struggles and pains; we lay tightly bound with each other. Lord Krishna is the string who holds us together; he is that simple, unseen thread!"

It was rejuvenating. She was witnessing it. The prayer-man was no less delighted; over the weeks he had started liking me, liking me for what was a question that I had no answer to.

Realization of dreams may not end up in their disappearance; they lay hidden for some time and re-emerge with more strength, I thought. A fulfilment does bring a surge of happiness, but is momentary. I was learning that I had to achieve peace not by any fulfilment, but by simply living a life accepting all occurrences and lapses.

And Shivani reinforced this thought in me. She was like an immense experience, not from this world, somewhere from the beyond. If I was afraid of this beyond, I would have left the scene immediately, but I stood there, waiting to understand more about this phenomenon. I had a desire, a seed hidden somewhere, of searching and longing to understand what lay beyond. A magnetic force like hers had caught me to orbit her. I had perhaps been waiting to meet her for many lives.

26

"Tomorrow, the day will begin with a purification bath; we hold leaves on our head and chant verses. The aim is to plead to the almighty for compassion and his blessings for all that one intends to do during the coming year. The seventh day of the month *Magha*, is a day on which the sun god turns his chariot drawn by seven horses. It is also his birthday," he said.

It was amazing to hear about sun god, my eyes sparkled with curiosity. By now, the prayer-man had got acclimatized to one-way conversations, as if he heard my questions coming from within.

"Are you wondering, what this chariot and seven horses is all about? The chariot of Sun has only one wheel, the *Kalachakra*, the wheel of time, and the seven horses represent seven colours of light. The Sun, the most evident illustration of His presence is the divine being dwelling in our hearts, pouring in his light and love, that determines the strength of our spirit and sensitivity. The Sun rules the heart, the right eye in men and the left eye in women. All our power of resistance and vitality comes from him. Now the chariot is actually metaphorical, it represents our mind. Innumerable thoughts arise and evolve within us; these are like different horses pulling us in diverse directions, but for our mind, we need to concentrate on the right kind of thoughts to move in the right directions. That is what celebration is all about tomorrow," he said.

"Wonderful Father, why do you not tell him a little about goddess earth too," I suddenly sensed a magnetic wave as Shivani interrupted our conversation by complimenting the prayer-man. She had come in with a vial of home-made medicine for me.

"Fortunately, we do not have the power to destroy the sun, he is too distant for us to do that, but the earth, despite being nurtured by her every moment, we have the audacity to trouble her as much as we can," he said with despair.

"Yes, it is time to reinforce the strength of goddess earth, but to do that we need to first restore our own energies," she said.

"But just as the sun provides us with his energies so does the earth and if we do not absorb all that she gives us, how can we restore ourselves."

"Yes, I agree with you, but we have lost that humility to acknowledge the energies that we receive from goddess earth; we have ended up taking her for granted like a child does with his mother," she said.

"You are right, we have stopped caring for her, she is the highest giver in our lives; we neither thank her nor acknowledge all that we receive from her. It is time we reinstated our connections with her.

"Yes, have you heard the story of Mother Earth when lord Krishna was to be born? She was so disgusted by the sins committed around her that she went to Lord Brahma, appealing to Him to do something about it. Lord Brahma appealed to lord Vishnu for help and then Lord Vishnu decided to take birth on Earth in the form of Lord Krishna."

"So do you think Mother Earth must be appealing to Lord Brahma even now?"

"I wish, Lord Krishna comes to us once again and comforts the earth."

"It is not Lord Krishna alone; god has bestowed on us the best of his qualities and expects us to do that rather than requesting Him to do it".

"Yes, I have seen you paying homage to Mother Earth, every morning before placing your feet on her."

"I apologize to her for all my wrong doings and thank her for all the good, and I do this *Prithvi Namaskar* everyday."

"Is Mother Earth the *Gayatri* that you talk about?"

"Yes, the *Gayatri*, but she has many names, *Bhoomi* is what the Buddha addressed her as when he achieved his enlightenment, she was the only witness."

27

Though all this while the prayer-man spoke to me and consoled himself that I understood him, my silent conversation with Shivani had assured him that I understood the language of the soul. Then onwards that had made him greatly vocal with me.

One day he made up his mind to speak to me about myself.

"It has been about four weeks now; you were brought here by my elder brother who found you lying unconscious at the end of the road outside the town. He saw that you were alive and felt that you will survive if given some care. That morning when you came, we called Rehman Bhai, our Hakim friend who has been looking after my family since the time my grandfather lived in this house, earlier it was his father who treated us and now he does." He kept on talking sometime about how Rehman Bhai has been kind to the family in different illnesses.

"First, Rehman Bhai was very worried and wanted to shift you to his home as he was nervous to see you in that state, but I assured him that both Satviki and I will look after you very well and help you regain your health." That day for the first time I came to know that the elderly woman who looked after me was his wife Satviki.

"Actually, my brother is a very good man, he is much elder to me, but is compassionate and kind. Years ago he lost his young son in an epidemic of cholera—an eighteen-year-old boy succumbed to it in a matter of six days. Since then he has been very lonely, he has been serving humanity with all his heart. When he saw you, he was reminded of his son and decided to save you." I was surprised that I had not seen this elder brother. He may or may not have come in four weeks time or may have visited me when I was asleep. In all conversations the prayer-man was trying to tell me about my state of illness.

"Rehman Bhai says that perhaps you lost your memory in an accident you had while coming to Gujranwala. After you regained consciousness, both Rehman Bhai and I tried to ask you who you were and if you recalled anything about what happened with you and how you reached at the end of the street. While your recovery from unconsciousness was nothing short of a miracle according to Rehman Bhai, he feels that you may revert to the mental condition of either your childhood or may not be able to recall anything of the past. But once you start speaking, there will be nothing wrong in starting your life all over again from the day you reached here," he comforted me with a smile.

"There was a deep injury on your temple, it has almost healed now, do you see the mark, I can show you, you can see it in the mirror;" he got up and placed a small mirror before me to show me the mark of the injury saying such injuries and their impact on the brain is very difficult to predict.

"The first few days, you only kept gazing blankly at Satviki and me, but I had told Satviki on the very first day that you will respond to our expressions in a very short time and you did," he just seemed so overwhelmed while telling me all this. I wondered who I was to him, but he had been so good to me unlike the people who had caused me this state.

"You spent much of your time looking at the children playing outside from the window," he said, which was true, I was so much at a loss about the place where I was living and the people who came in to see me.

Benazir Patil

"Satviki was very happy to see you eating the food that she prepared for you with great interest, because we do not know where you come from and what your food habits are; you definitely are not from Gujranwala?" he questioned me and there I was, again with no answers.

"But I know that you understand what we talk with you, now I am confident of that, do you not feel like saying something?" he was coaxing me to say something and there was absolutely nothing wrong in doing that. He had been patiently waiting to hear something from me, initially the eagerness may have been with regard to my whereabouts, but later it looked like he was just eager that I talked and started interacting and leading a normal life. I could not recall anything about the incident, the unconsciousness, or my initial blankness.

Though I had returned to life, what direction I should take was unclear. I looked at myself as a completely new person. I had got attached to the prayer-man and his family but they were essentially just strangers. Every morning, I woke up with no idea what I was to do. The memory of who I was seemed to have been forever locked away somewhere.

The prayer-man was helping me create a new lifetime to cherish in the coming years.

28

There was nothing that I was seeking; I had even lost the understanding of the creator, if there was a creator, so much so good for him to have created all of us, if people feared him and kept away from sins, that was even better, if they contemplated of heaven and hell, that was also wonderful, but I was not concerned with any of these.

Despite all this, I was deeply in love with life. Life's every direction appeared to me like moving towards a celebration. In that isolation I was deeply connected to someone.

"Your *atman* is your whole world; your soul is intact in your body for you have a task to fulfil." Shivani's words reverberated volubly.

The cause of my living had to be found, my pristine soul had to be deciphered. Searching for everything else was a detour, getting lost midway, ignoring the thirst of understanding the vicinity, and fearing the suffering to come; all was meaningless till I understood who I was. I was meeting fellow beings every now and then; I was not sure if they were all seeking to understand their purpose on this earth, but I was glad that they definitely had a purpose in my life, of holding my hand and taking me on the path that could help me unfold my mind.

I placed my hands on my chest to feel more about what I was going through: Shivani would say, "there lays the heart chakra, the place which controls love and compassion in us." Strangely, she was right, I could feel my heart, and I could feel it was overflowing with love. I lifted my hand and placed it on my head, which she referred to as crown chakra, the place which manifested our spiritual connection with the universe.

But what had made me most curious was the third eye she often talked about, the place on the forehead between the two eyes. I had always seen Satviki with a coloured dot on her third eye and I wondered the reason for it. I could not recall if I had ever seen women with this in the past. But I definitely felt that there was some connection I had with this third eye. I tried hard to recall what it was and could only reach an understanding that it had something to do with our relation with Mother Earth. This thought had been lingering on my mind since the time I had heard the prayer-man and Shivani talking about restoring our connection with her.

What a strange life I was living. I was striving hard to move my mind from the pleasure of everything that I was seeing to all that was unseen and unknown. I had no affections and desires, a freedom from these had come naturally; the only stumbling block, which was proving grievous, was the distance between my soul and the contemplation of the divine. With no understanding of sorrows and adversities, I found it difficult to understand happiness and pleasure too.

But the greatest thing to happen to me was love. I did not need to understand or dig out either my past or future; there was no question of understanding whether I had been through it before. That alone had lightened all my burdens.

Several times had I seen the book wrapped with yellow satin: I did uncover it, turned pages after pages, tried to read it, the script seemed alien, yet it was revealing something. The feeling that the book had been with me for long was getting stronger.

Finally I opened it, Page 7 read:

Suffering meant seven things in human life:

> *It comes with a purpose*

> *It toughens*

> *It cleanses*

> *It liberates*

> *It generates faith*

> *It alleviates*

> *And it is atonement*

Suffering extends seven messages:

The harder you hit, the deeper it goes. When life hammers you, rejoice not in the pain of the strike but in the depth of its effect.

We cannot heal ourselves if we do not release the hurt from within.

If you want to see the brave, look to those who can return love for hatred. If you want to see the heroic, look to those who can forgive.

"Live in joy", it is not necessary to be loyal to your suffering.

Humans use their finite knowledge to determine whether something is good or bad. In our ignorance, we conclude that what we perceive is what is correct. However, the truth is, whatever we think is bad, may possibly be a good thing. No one truly knows the true nature of things that happen but The All Wise, The Creator.

The messiah suffered 7 wounds, 2 in the palms, 2 in the wrists, 2 in the feet and 1 on the side.

Your suffering will be your greatest guide.

I knew this language; I may have learned it, wondered who had taught me and from where this book had reached my hands.

*It is not time or opportunity that is to determine intimacy;
it is disposition alone. Seven years would be insufficient to
make some people acquainted with each other, and seven days
are more than enough for others.*

Jane Austen

29

"You leave him my son, you just leave him," Shamsher said with a slightly raised voice.

"I know you have no desire to possess his wealth, but he will not understand, only I can comprehend your inner self, you will find very few people who will understand the language of love, the words of concern, you must leave him, you and I do not possess the capacity to change this materialistic world, from antiquity this universe has witnessed such doubts and misgivings, it has witnessed the cruelties of a brother to his brother, of son to his father and of fellowmen to their fellowmen, you and I are no exception!" Shamsher expressed with utter despair.

I woke up from my sleep; I was panting, as if I had been running for years, the sweat on my brows and in my palms was a mere sign of some fear. Was it a nightmare? Or did my soul drift into another world as my body slept? I had perhaps walked into this bright light from some dark street. My fear was not causeless, neither was it my imagination. I recalled those moments of fear, and felt fortunate for being blessed with the ability to understand it.

I sensed a jolt in my entire being; I looked at my feet, confidently placed on the earth, brightened by a queer agility, I reconnected myself to the fearless Khudabakhsh I had always been. Fear, I definitely lived with when I craved for feeling sheltered, when I looked for a certain tomorrow, a lasting relationship and an inescapable wisdom. But Zeba's departure had taught me that neither of these was available to anyone, and I would soon experience the mysterious future overflowing with relations that were transient and knowledge that was evolving.

I sat aghast for a moment, without realizing what was happening to me. The open eyes and the memories of the past conflicted. I closed my eyes to see if I could still connect with my disconnected dream, and there I was, one conversation after the other took me back to the unpleasant reality. Everything that had happened months ago in Bamiyan cascaded down my senses. I was as fresh as ever with the thoughts of Mir Raza and Shamsher. In my journey from Hamadan to Bamiyan, that had not just been my longest stay but my closest bond in the last seven years.

I had learned the trade from Mir Raza, I had acquired all the skills that he had, his strength of convincing people to engage in business, his skill to negotiate, his tact of managing the servants. Slowly, I had learned to dress up like him, all the people world over who came to meet us walked out with an indubitable credence that I was his brother. Mir Raza too was soaring high with the roaring business and never felt uncomfortable about my presence and my ways of working. Sometimes, he travelled far and wide to bring more business and I managed everything for Shamsher as well as the business single-handedly.

Shamsher often expressed amazement at Mir Raza's trust in me and reiterated, "I must confess you have done some magic on my son, it is not in his nature to trust people so easily, and least to trust someone in business."

I also felt happy that I was learning so much and was a helping hand to Mir Raza.

One evening Mir Raza had returned from his business trip to Khorasan. He looked distressed and annoyed about

Benazir Patil

something, both Shamsher and I tried to quest as to what untoward had happened but there was no response from him.

The next day onwards I found him talking to me with a strange sense of mockery.

Matters escalated to the extent that he confronted me in the presence of Shamsher.

"You think you can capture my world of business, don't you?" he asked me with anger and continued without waiting for my response.

"I thought you were different, but greed has finally overcome you, possessions and riches have become your life and now you have no two thoughts about taking away all the property that I have hard-earned in the last many years!"

I was absolutely unaware of what he was talking about and so was Shamsher. Shamsher had been more shocked than I. He tried to intervene and ask Mir Raza what had caused him this misunderstanding, but Mir Raza did not budge from his attitude and opinion. He accused me of having stolen a large chunk of earnings that had come from a businessman in Bukhara and shared that it was by chance he had been able to find this out; he also thought that I had been siphoning off a lot of it in his absence.

"I can never play the game of money, my brother, I possess nothing at all and I do not intend to possess anything ever, here you can check all I have with me, I gather that your fears and doubts are coming from elsewhere, they do not seem to be owned by you, you have been highly mistaken. I take care of your business just like I take care of your father. I have lived here with no motives of building my future," I responded.

I had learned to deal with the gains and losses in business. Every time I faced a loss, Shamsher Raza would convince me that it is a part of the game and I should not expect to be successful in every deal I struck. After each new loss, my mind would work even harder to compensate for the same in the next deal. Perseverance in gaining wealth had become one of my qualities. Though I knew that I had nothing to do with all the riches, but I had started enjoying the game of materialistic earning. But that day, Mir Raza's accusations had caused me severe pain; I had not grieved like that anytime in my life before, I was at a complete loss to understand myself. I searched for my calmness and had found it difficult to bring it back. My real peace had departed from me much earlier than I thought. What I was living with was a misty veil of success.

I suddenly felt that it was pointless to argue with Mir Raza about my innocence.

"Here, my brother, I came with nothing to you and today I leave with nothing," I told Mir Raza.

"No, my son!" exclaimed Shamsher and continued with a saddened face: "You have been kindest to us in the times of our need, you have looked after me like you would your own father. I ask Mir Raza to get into the depth of what has happened and I vouch for your sincerity to him, do not leave like this and do not convince him too, it is not in your hands to do that, the almighty will convey the truth to him in his own ways."

"I understand your emotions; I leave with no grudge in my heart, but blessings to Mir Raza that he is able to grasp the truth one day. If almighty wills I will come back to you one day." Saying so, I quietly bid farewell to them.

Benazir Patil

Tiredness grew inside me, suddenly my journey had lost its direction, my mind turned gloomy and I knew not what anxiety had overpowered me. If I had not possessed anything, what loss was I grieving about? My mind was too tired to investigate the cobwebs within.

As I walked out of the palatial mansion, I looked at the radiant twilight percolating its calmness. After pondering for some time, my mind quivered. I prostrated to Mother Earth, I tried to hear and hear for a long time, I could hear nothing at all. Mother Earth had robbed me of my sensations. In the last many days, I had forgotten to listen to her, I had ignored her emotions and had squandered away my time in calculating the gains and losses; she too had kept away from transmitting her sentiments to me. Had I committed a sin? As I started nursing disapproval of myself, I was reminded of Shamsher's words, he had rightly said, earning riches for oneself was easy, but giving it up after having earned it was the real test. I was glad I had learnt the reality about myself the hard way. Within a short period god had brought me back to my senses. I rejoiced in the realization. My grief was slowly turning into gratitude and happiness. Re-starting my journey, I meditated on my doings; I was soon blooming again like a flower, calmness and peace hovering around me like butterflies. I looked at the setting sun, filled myself with the energies it was transmitting and prostrated to Mother Earth once again. The consciousness that I treasured my relationship with her more than anything set into me. All else seemed unimportant, even the injustice and the humiliation I had been through. I shared the feeling of hurt with her and like a small child I confessed how I understood god's purpose behind it. My injured self was but an adverse response to the unanticipated happenings.

"God has created human beings in His own image, pardon the one who has injured you. Be as generous as the Almighty in liberating your fellow beings from the burden of their purposeful and unintentional doings," I heard her saying.

I learned that I could release myself from the impact of discomforting incidents through the innate abilities god had bestowed me with. The strength to forgive was one of them. I was tempted to go back to Shamsher and Mir Raza to thank them for the greatest insight I had arrived at. I contemplated on turning back; just then something heavy hit me on my head. For a few moments I thought some outrageous thugs were hunting me. I felt some blood rolling down my forehead and suddenly everything turned blank.

Benazir Patil

30

Daybreak seemed a few hours away, I stood near my bed, looking outside the window, and recuperating from the lost identity I lived with. Everything that had taken place came gushing to my mind.

Every incident in my life was introducing me to the stranger within, encouraging me to comprehend the fact that our birth is not just some distinct episode; it is a process that we go through during the course of our life till we cease to exist as an earthly phenomenon. During this process, I recognized things that I could understand, but I also found things I could not understand. Strangest were the ones I did not come to know I could not understand. And the unambiguous fearlessness had come to wake with this one; it had emanated from the faith in the divine, and the intimacy I had developed with Mother Earth.

Ironically, living through this process, I had reached yet another unknown interval, where I had no past and no identity. Fortunately, I was saved from being reborn; I had been returned my memory that allowed me to continue with the same birth, with the same name and known emotions. I was happy to find myself again, happier to realize that I did not run away from my past and happiest to have learned that in the finality of our lives, we will not be measured by the standards of our civilization, but by the standards of our faith.

I sat on the ground and without any thought prostrated to Mother Earth. I lay there for some time, I stood up, sat by the small window, in complete silence, watching the stars tracing their path and changing their positions.

After an hour, since no sleep had come over my eyes, I stood up, paced to and fro, and walked out of the room. I looked back inside, through the same small window; there stood Shivani, tranquil, arms folded, radiance dazzling through her whole being. A strange anxiety overtook me; I came back to my room.

I had moved into one world from another, from one of oblivion to that of illusion.

Suddenly, my thoughts went back to Shamsher.

"We are never at home in this world; we are consciously trying to re-create everything around us. Even if there exists no conflict with all that we live, we still aspire to make those things to look different and an acceptance of the way things are is rather unacceptable," he often told me.

Success was also one such thing perhaps, defining our own path, relying upon our confidence to change things gradually becomes a passion. It all starts with longing, moves on to a path comprising a combination of satisfaction and dissatisfaction, developing into a refusal to accepting failure. And then the vice is neither lust, nor hatred, nor vanity, jealousy nor envy, but pure despair.

I had refused to work with Mir Raza, justifying myself that I did not have a passion for making money. But Shamsher had encouraged me to join him by rightly saying, "To give up a temptation in life you have to earn that luxury and test yourself if you have the heart to remain detached."

It was now I was realizing that it is not easy to assess where one stands and fathom the depth of obstacles created in the course of one's spiritual growth. A human mind happily falls prey to tempting achievements and does not want to part from them. Reaching this point of self-realization, the ability

Benazir Patil

to remain detached, was a blessing I was not accustomed to before being with Shamsher and Mir Raza

⊷⟨⊱⟩⊷

Different things had arrived from different people, my mind wandered back to Shosyos and Shah Baba. But the freshest in my mind was the conversation between Shivani and the prayer-man, about the seven temptations.

"How can we reduce our needs?"

"Only when we stop asking, stop standing with our open hands, we have to become doers. We have been put here for each other not for ourselves. "Have you heard the story of lunching in heaven and hell?" she asked.

"No, what is that?"

"Once there was a man, who felt frustrated when nobody could explain to him the difference between heaven and hell. Seeing his frustration, one night god himself walked into his dream and took him along to explain the difference: they both stood near the first chamber, people inside were waiting for lunch with long spoons in their hands. Then they moved to the second chamber, there too, people were waiting for food with the same long spoons in their hands. God looked at the man and said, the first chamber was hell and the second heaven. But the man wondered and queried to god how that was possible since there was no difference at all, they all looked the same, waiting eagerly for food. God took him for another round to see how they were lunching together: in the first chamber they saw that the people were trying their best to eat with the long spoons, but they couldn't put even a few crumbs into their mouth and were crying out of frustration; then they moved to the second chamber and saw that people were using the same long spoons to feed each other and were rejoicing in doing that."

"Wonderful! But how can we ever give up on something like food?"

"The food we eat should be the one needed for our bodies. There is a lot that is meant as food for our soul, we have to seek that more than what we seek for our bodies. A smile with gratitude is food for the soul than the body."

"And what about the need for our happiness?"

"We grow happier and become more beautiful when we cast a loving look at someone. We meet others, we see things, we love and feel loved, we walk, we talk, we begin and end each day, but how often do we ponder and cherish the gift of giving happiness than receiving happiness."

"So we can never give up our need to express our feelings?"

"We notice the change of day and night, months and years, seasons and climate, but we rarely notice our storms and thunders within. When we commit a mistake, we want to be forgiven, but when someone else does that we want him to be punished; our feelings are just like that, sympathy for self and bias towards others."

"And what about our possessiveness for all those we love?"

"You possess your loved ones and do not want to depart from them; you do not want to give them their own life but want them to grow under your love and comfort and never want them to grow as per their wishes and plans. You possess them not as your love, but as your wealth."

Benazir Patil

"And what about the need for achievement and status?"

"We fear the unknown future, we fear our needs of tomorrow; this is the reason why we accumulate wealth for our needs."

Whenever we feel, we can retire into ourselves, to be at rest and to be free from all businesses. We cannot retire better than to our own soul.

"And what about the need for love?"

"You have separated yourself from your love like the waves of the ocean. Unveil your hearts and spirits and see that the cups of desire that we are carrying can only get filled with devotion and generosity, how much ever you try hard selfishness and wants will only deplete the contents of it. As a child you were taught the lessons of love, but today you seem to have forgotten them."

"It is a strange situation, a speechless love cries aloud to you, a wingless love continues to fly to you, and a forceless love embraces you gently."

"But what about the possessiveness for our children?"

"You were born a child and as a child you did not calculate, you gave what you had, you rarely had fears of losing anything, you did not understand much about possessing, you always felt secured at the thought of asking your parents and had this faith that they are there in your life to give you what you wanted."

"You grew up and learned to calculate, accommodated the fears of losing what you had by giving it to others, you nurtured your ego, you lost faith in the capability of your parents to give you what you wanted, because now your dreams and longings were not to have small, beautiful and priceless things, but to have big and priced things, and eventually you lost the security and the heart to give, and you could never agree and wish to part from anything."

"You say that you have memories of your childhood and you long to go back to those days. I say it is not you who longs for it, it is those memories and those days that long for you, they long and you resist."

"You possess your children and do not want to give them, you do not want to give them their own life, you teach them, groom them and you just love to see them growing, you not only want them to be happy but you are willing to give up your own happiness to see their smiles and you just cannot stand their tears, but gradually you start treating them like your wealth from which you cannot part and then you want them to be the way you desire."

I had fallen in love with her.

Clad always in white, a distinct feature of hers, reminded me of someone.

White, the source of all colors, 'abyad' in the holy book meant radiance and purity. Her white attire symbolized her pious influence on my mind; it embodied the commencement of my path.

Benazir Patil

31

Things had changed gradually in those few weeks; the whitewashed houses around in the hustle-bustle of the mornings came across as faces smiling at each other. In due course, passers-by who peeped into my window had become my friends by virtue of the pleasant glances we exchanged. The foliage of perfumed jasmine brought in a pleasant feel all through the mansion. An unacknowledged stare at me was a rarity. There was nothing as winsome as that voyage where the soul within me and the souls outside me remained unknown and yet I enjoyed the silent companionship of both.

The sun would go down, pulling out its last ray from entering my window and the night would bring its incensed aroma. Never before had I so intensely observed these charms of nature. I had become acquainted with its sounds and recitals. A battle with my own memory had not led to a defeat, but to a freedom from most of the worlds I had lived in. The ardent urge to escape from that state had slowly disappeared.

Hopes suddenly got justified as I went on speaking anxiously to myself. The interval that seemed like an age had come to an end. A strong magnetism seized me, resistance turning into delight. But was I a victor? Where was I reaching? A sensible me was watching the dawn that was coming up slowly. Few hours had passed since the time the stranger inside me had revealed his identity.

Last so many days I constantly heard the footsteps of the prayer-man walking up to me. My discourses with him were silent but regular; his care had instilled a strange courage inside me. He only examined me with his kind eyes, never questioned me. Never did he speak of my unresponsive and blank state. His glances always conveyed a deep sense of comfort laden with simple fondness.

I had slowly become familiar with all the souls who visited the prayer-man's family. Some were simple and childlike, some were businessmen, some seemed alien, but most of them admired Shivani and talked about her as a blessed child. I often felt them like my own family, free from vanities and desires, who looked at me with love and understanding, telling me that I was even worthy of their veneration.

I had evolved into a sincere listener. Whether it was grief, yearning, laughter or rage, all of it was entwined, interrelated and enriching to my ears. Everything together, all suffering and all pleasure had become my world. When I neither heard the lamentations nor the laughter, I felt as if I was not tied to all those souls around. Though I had awakened to the tragic nightmare that I had been through after being hit mercilessly by those unknown men, the glimpses of that dreadful act had faded away in the beauteous moments I had spent with the prayer-man's family.

Truly, man had learned to complain about the thorns with the rose, but in reality, was it not a boon that the thorns actually had something as wonderful as a rose. Had it not been for that tragic event I would not have reached this wonderful place. Throughout my life I had questioned the purpose of every destination that I had reached. But this time I knew that I had reached here for a strange reason. The seven weeks had been like seven nights of wonderful sleep filled with dreams that had rejuvenated my entire soul. I felt fully awake.

Drenched in my own thoughts, my eyes noticed a small wooden table and a wardrobe: it meant someone had been

Benazir Patil

living here before I occupied the place. The books on the table looked old and had been referred to several times. I picked one of the books and dusted off little mud particles that had gathered on it. My silence was broken by my mind's own voice; I was able to narrate to myself what was written in the book, it was the *Ketaab-e-Hayaat* that I always carried with me since the time Daniyaal had handed it over to me.

I opened it randomly as I had done in the past, but refrained from reading it, I was reminded of the last page I had read before I left Mir Raza's house and subsequently slipped into this disorientation. Shamsher's pleading to wait had caused a bit of emotional upheaval: it was not the attachment with him that was troubling me, it was the pain in his eyes that had made me uncomfortable. Completely distressed, I opened the *Ketaab-e-Hayaat,* those last words referred to changing the seven detestable traits in us to seven enchanting qualities.

> *Transforming the Solar vanity into humility*
> *Transforming the Lunar greed into generosity*
> *Transforming the Venusian lust into chastity*
> *Transforming the Martian wrath into affection*
> *Transforming the Mercurian indolence into perseverance*
> *Transforming the Saturnian voracity into self-restraint*
> *And*
> *Transforming the Jupiterian jealousy into compassion*

Surprised at my own sense of recall, I wondered if anybody around would have believed I possessed an iota of strength to even recall what had happened on the previous day. I drifted into the endless memories, the list was never-ending, everything was gradually falling into place, I realized I could recollect all of my twenty-one years.

Eagerly, I turned the pages of the book once again and opened Page 160, it read:

> The seven rays of energy from the space entwine to build a reality:
>
> The first ray is that of will and power and wisdom,
>
> The second ray, virtually, the energy of the enture solar system,
>
> The third ray, natural intellectual ideation in pursuit of truth,
>
> The fourth ray stimulates creativity, art and beauty,
>
> The fifth ray is of concrete knowledge and science,
>
> The sixth ray is the ray of devotion,
>
> The seventh ray is the ray of organization and ritual.

With every word that I read I was drawing parallels with the man that existed inside me.

My eagerness knew no bounds, as I continued reading about the seven rays, I recalled what Shivani had said about the seven chakras in human body, her efforts to heal the heart chakra in my body, and its connectivity to different rays of sun.

I ardently waited for the morning to arrive.

32

An overwhelming respite filled my senses; a calming faith in the goodness of humanity had come alive once again. I heard the prayer-man's footsteps once again. He was no more a stranger to me because I was no stranger to myself anymore. I inspected his face; I knew him; an urge to talk to him about myself surged through my mind like lightening.

Motionless stood the prayer-man in front of me for a moment.

"*Om Tat Sat,*" he came near me and whispered into my ears as usual.

I felt as if I had known him for years. My connection with him was yet another manifestation of my fortune.

"Is this a prayer that you pour into my soul?" I asked him in a blend of Persian—cum-Urdu that I had picked up quite naturally while I lived with Shamsher.

He looked at me, startled but happy. Efficiently hiding the expression of surprise, he responded with natural affection.

"Yes, my son, it is the truth of our lives that the lord wants us to know," he responded with utmost delight, filled with gratification that the prayer had worked.

"'*Om*' is the root of all sounds that continues to vibrate within and without; '*Tat*' is the supreme lord, the source of the entire universe, and '*Sat*' is the reality, the creator. '*Tat*' is the transcendent, the otherworldly, impossible to grasp, beyond the reaches of space and time. It symbolizes the omnipresence of God, the aboveness is *Tat,* the hereness is *Sat,* and the everywhereness is *Om.*

I too heard it with complete oneness with the almighty and smiled back.

"What comes to your mind?" he asked me.

"I only remember that I had walked for a few miles in Bamiyan and was hit by someone from behind; it was indeed an irony that the thieves had considered me a rich businessman and had attacked me."

I explained to him about my incessant journey from Hamadan to his house, the plans to visit Fatehpur and my *parwaaz* after Zeba's death.

"I had left Hamadan to reach where destiny wanted to take me. I had refrained from forcing my naïve soul to do anything that would unnerve the people who loved me, but walking from one place to another was not in my hands, my path was guided by some force," I concluded.

"You can be with us as long as you want to, nursing you to a good health has been a pleasure, seeing you full of life again is indeed wonderful," he said.

I was awfully delighted by the beautiful conversation I was having with the prayer-man. But my mind seemed a little lost; I was asking myself if Shivani would also be keen to know who I was and where I came from: would she be curious to know where I was heading? would she be longing for me just the way I longed for her? I was not fleeing from anything, nor was I able to settle down. For a moment I felt

Benazir Patil

as if the saintly soul inside her had already gauged the truth about me; however, I was still keen to tell her.

"Shivani does not seem to be around," I could not resist and finally asked the prayer-man.

"She has left for Lahore to live with my ailing sister for a few days."

My mind ached; I had not imagined that the day of meeting would turn out to be a day of parting for me. There was a time when I was a seeker of silence and then there was a time when I wanted to break out of my silence. I knew not what to speak; I only knew that I was deeply in love with her. My speechlessness despite regaining of speech was a reflection of the truth that I had not been able to fathom the deeper secrets of my heart myself.

My heart was not aware of its own depth until it experienced the torment of parting.

"Time will go by and I shall not mind this either," I could barely console myself.

With much patience I looked at the *Ketaab-e-Hayaat*, picked it up, opened Page 25, it read.

> *There are ten primary numbers:*
>> *One is the basis of all*
>> *Four, six, eight, nine and ten are produced by multiplying some of these numbers*
>> *Two, three, four and five produce some of these primary numbers*
>> *Seven neither produces any nor is produced; isolation is in its nature.*

33

Satviki often exchanged words on how the world progressed, very often it was about the differences that were emanating in the communities that had lived together peacefully for centuries. All through my life, I had only heard and read about wars, I may have been in the midst of it too but did not go through its strife. I had witnessed humans discriminating against humans in the worst possible ways. Perhaps, Satviki was also witnessing some struggle around her.

"People all over the world have always had some differences I feel, but differences based on religious ideologies have been the most pathetic but severe," she said to me one day.

"Yes, but have we not seen that as much human beings have fought about, they have also managed to cling together?" I questioned her.

"Probably, that may be true; we all have grown opposing each other about every basic aspect we deal with. Within our families, within the relationships outside, within our countries and within our religions, we have opposed and come together, always, at-least that is what I have been through in last so many years. We don't want to live with each other and yet we live happily with each other," she said.

"I agree with you, the reality is right here, a lot of us are still willing to live with differences and respect the differences that we are born with and possess so dearly," I said.

"Yes Khuda," she sighed, "but this picture is becoming a little grim. To me these differences are looking different, they do not seem to be like before, I wonder where it will lead to, I cannot see anything good coming out of it and I fear the worse that may soon emerge as a truth," she exclaimed with dejection.

"Over the centuries, many differences in human beings had deepened thoroughly, fear and ignorance had got merged with each other and had pulled humanity away from the natural world," I added.

"Strangely, nations are entering into empty glories; the carnage of wars and the loss of human lives are making people weep in unseen silence, death and destruction have become the only means of achievement," said Satviki.

"The soldiers stake their lives to guard their motherland. Circumstances force them to kill, they are expected to destroy their enemies, but after all, enemies are humans too," I murmured to myself.

"There is no certainty that they will return home; they are unsure about whether they will be able to be with their families when their families need them," she immediately complemented to what I had said.

I understood where she was coming from, but a word of agreement on this would have made her more nervous. All the same, I was myself not convinced that humanity was to die a death so easily.

One morning, I found Satviki eagerly waiting for me; her expressions conveyed that she had something serious to share.

"I had often dreamt of my death, the first time was twenty years ago," she expressed to me with great intensity as if I could predict if it would come true.

"Dreaming of death means extension of life, that's the way people understand back in my hometown," I responded with a smile

"May be, but, the first time it had upset me intensely; the whole day the dream had ruminated in my mind along with anxiety of sharing it with someone I could confide in. I had heard from my granny that one should go and share the bad dreams with someone so that they don't come true," she shared with utmost innocence.

"I had heard about dreams from my aunts and cousins, it was always a lot of fun to hear about each one's dreams and then what really followed after that. One of my aunts even narrated about what things in the dreams symbolized what actions and happenings in life; these discussions occurred mostly during the weddings and post family functions when everybody got together. But many of these things were mere superstitions and everyone loved to drift into the talks about demons and spirits," she said.

I remembered my conversation with Daniyaal.

God has secret ways of talking to his children. In one parable, Jesus said, "the knowledge of the secrets of the kingdom . . ." Thus it meant that god gave secrets to all those who are eager to learn more. The fact that god gives us dreams shows that He wants all of us to learn more than the mind can reveal.

"And what do you understand by these dreams?"

Benazir Patil

"You see many things when you dream; you may have seen fish and snakes too!"

"I cannot believe it! How do you know this?"

"We all see it, fish are generally a good omen, and snakes signify an inner strength, a step towards spiritual awakening."

She seemed to suddenly fall into deep thoughts, she looked at me with a strange curiosity in her eyes and said, "and what does it mean when you see your death?"

"Death in a dream, especially your own, suggests that it is time for you to let go something that you have been clinging to, it also means your growth and in no way indicates the end of your life."

"And have you ever dreamt of angels?"

"Yes I have, why are you asking?"

"I once dreamt of an angel, I was dying and the angel stood by my bed, after the dream I continued to recall as often as possible to understand who that angel was but in vain."

"How would you recall the face of an angel?"

"Because the angel was familiar."

"Familiar? Tell me more," I uttered with interest.

"I finally decided to settle my mind and that I should no more think of it. But the more I tried to escape, the more I got pulled into it. While I was still adjusting with this escape mechanism, it suddenly struck me that I had seen an image around me while I lay on deathbed; it was an image of an angel. And then I kept on going back and forth to my dream to recall more about the angel I had seen. The incessant effort to recollect the image of the angel gradually overpowered my thoughts of death," she said.

Satviki was telling me exactly what I understood about the human mind.

As children we get conditioned to experiencing emotions, we are taught to do this right from our very first breath, and the lessons continue as we grow. There comes a time when we take pride in experiencing these emotions. Though we are taught that happiness is the most worthy out of the whole lot, we also want to identify with others, because unless we experience pain and despair, we will never sense the charm of happiness. I started believing very early that it was not just about that, it was equally a reality that apart from happiness I wanted to feel pain and understand what hurts me, because that gave me more insights about who I was and what affected me.

"My inner self was signaling me that this was not just an inconsequential dream, there was something about it, and it was connected to something in my existing life. Rather the dream was connected to my life and not to my death!" she said.

"The dream had awakened me. There was a sense of mindfulness. I was reminded of the Buddha, as I had become conscious of every little thought," she said.

"I am reminded of Shosyos, my friend who explained to me more about the Buddha," I interrupted.

"What did he tell you?" she questioned with eagerness.

Benazir Patil

"That the transitory nature of life was one of the chief causes of our suffering."

"Tell me what you understood from it."

"Yes, but let us talk about your dream first," I said.

"We will, but I am more keen to hear about the Buddha," Satviki always expressed eagerness to hear more about my understanding of concepts. Perhaps that is why she had decided to share about her dream with me.

"The dimensions of this suffering are dual in nature: one aspect is parting from what one possesses; the second is not getting what one wants. Suffering does not stop here, however; it has one more attachment to it—fear—and this fear is very strange: when one does not possess what one wants, there is a fear of not getting it at all, so ideally it means that when people finally possess what they want, the fear factor should disappear, but this does not happen, because after possessing something human beings live with the fear of losing it. And so fear is always walking parallel with suffering." I paused and continued.

"The suffering again, is not related to the self alone, it has a lot to do with the relationships one has with others, because one cannot isolate oneself from others and be selfish in some things and not be selfish in others, so finally selfishness is also visible and manifested in the relationships people have in their lives. So much so that human beings start treating their fellow beings also as materialistic possessions—like non-living things. Apart from this, if any other fellow being affects or is not favorable to the process of one's desires and achievements, everything else becomes immaterial and the prime factor that emerges is how to get rid of that relationship," I said.

"Could there be a desire that may not affect others around us?" she questioned.

"For humans, the urge to fulfill a desire is not a wish or a desire alone, it gets bundled with envy, jealousy and, at times, into enmity, though all of us feel humble and accept that our needs and desires are justified and it has nothing to do with snatching anything from anybody, and that our intentions are glorified by means which are pure and legitimate, such as hard work and persuasion. The same intentions become wild and harmful when we experience blocks in achieving our desires. When we see people as hurdles, we try hard to annihilate even the living beings around us. Yet we do not stop at this alone: once a particular desire is fulfilled, it is not the end; it leads to a want for more, making the list of our wishes and desires endless. Our ego becomes the prime aspect of our lives and we get conditioned to fulfilling our egos," I concluded.

"This was enlightening, Khuda; now let me tell you more about my dream," she said with a smile.

"One morning, as I heard the sound of *azaan* in the waking hours of the day, I was startled by the vision I got: I could once again see the angel standing near my bed, smiling at me. Familiar and enchanting smile it was. While the eyes still remain closed, I embarked my mind with a question of who the angel was. With much desire I chased the vision and went back in time to see if I knew the angel. Anxiety was up to its brim. Just then, my mind collided with the memories of the time when Shivani was to be born. Six days before her birth, a strange old *dervish* stood on the doorstep of my house. I was tired for the day and had no heart to come out and talk to him, but I felt as if he wanted something and so I took some grains of rice from one of the containers and walked to the gate. He looked at me and said, 'I do not want

Benazir Patil

anything, just wanted to tell you that the birth of your child is going to change your life, your child will go miles ahead of you and will be known for her goodness and love for this world!' and he walked away," said Satviki.

"Shivani was born. Her adventures filled volumes, a nascent child with a constant quest for something. At the age where every human being is stuck between the two extremes—a life harassed by wants and a life that is completely free from wants—she had arrived at a mode in which there was harmony between the mind and the heart. As a child she had attained this harmony where the mind did not dictate the ends of life, but only helped to attain those ends that were dictated by the heart. Contentment was visible in every word she spoke and it felt like a lasting happiness on her face, which actually came from the freedom she had gained from all worldly desires."

"Shivani's strangeness had started standing out. I realized that people around, be it neighbours, friends or relatives, who interacted with her would find her different and would generally be more curious about what she said in response to various questions."

"But who was that angel in your dream?" I interrupted.

"When Shivani was about six years old," she started again without paying heed to my question, "a *dervish* clad in black robes stood at the gate of the garden and called for Shivani."

"*Beti, O beti!*"

"Shivani walked up to the gate without any hesitation and responded to him,"

'Yes *baba*, what do you want?'

'I am a wanderer, one of my friends asked me to travel with him to Oonjha, I went with him, I got so lost there that I did not feel like coming back, but one day I thought of you and felt that I should come and meet you,' "the *dervish* replied," said Satviki.

"Her father realized that Shivani was conversing with an unknown voice and he rushed to the door; he was startled to find her talking to the *dervish* in such a friendly manner, he immediately pulled Shivani away and angrily asked the *dervish* what he was up to."

"*Bhai,* I know your daughter. I had come to your house just a few days before she was to be born and I had spoken to your wife about it," the *dervish* replied with a smile. I was overhearing the conversation from the kitchen, my curiosity heightened the moment the *dervishes* voice fell on my ears. I almost rushed, I had not really observed his face when I had met him last, but his words and voice was much accumulated in my memory as if I had heard him just yesterday. For the first time I had met a *dervish* who was not interested in taking alms but was keen to tell me about the child that was growing in my womb. At the back of beyond I always thought that he never came back to enquire about the baby girl he had spoken about. Reaching the scene, I recognized the *dervish* and indicated to Shivani's father that I knew him and there was nothing to fear about, though he rarely showed interest in such people and was fully aware that I was always inclined to talking to them thinking they were Sufis, and were closer to god," she said.

"But what was Shivani conversing with the *dervish*?" I asked her.

"I then turned to Shivani to ask her what she was telling the *dervish*."

She responded, 'I was telling him why he did not come to meet me all these years.'

"I was shocked for a moment, as I was about to react. I immediately took charge of her wits and gathered that perhaps Shivani's spiritual powers had given her an inkling of the *dervish* and his discussions with her. Her father's inquisitiveness knew no bounds, but something inside him held him back as he continued observing the discussions between the three of us," she said.

"Marveled by the fact that Shivani already knew about the *dervish*, I stood quietly and continued to hear the conversation between the two. The *dervish* told Shivani, *'beti,* there is so much in your mind, please do not hold; Allah wants you to share everything that you feel with the outside world. As you grow up, the world's distressed lot will walk up to you to unravel what it is that has created miseries in their lives; your words will not just soothe them but will direct them to a path that will help them reach the divine,'" Satviki said and took a long pause.

"But who was that angel in your dream?" I questioned again.

"That still remains a mystery, Khuda" she responded.

⟡

Positioning her simplicity before me, Satviki had often led me into tales of curiosity and concentration. That day too she caught me glancing at her and wanted to understand the intensity of my thought process but I sat before her overwhelmed. I rose, and requested her to follow me to the courtyard. As she came along I asked her to stop and signalled her to observe me. She obeyed with no hesitation. I prostrated on the ground for a moment and asked her to do the same. She surprisingly glanced at the sky above and reacted as if it was something to do with the climate . . .

She smiled at me prostrated on the ground and waited for further instructions. After a few minutes I said, "get up if you feel like, but if not please continue and concentrate on your inner thoughts; if you can move away from your own thoughts, then concentrate on all that is reaching your mind at this very moment."

"Ok, Khuda let me try," she said without lifting her head. I sat still with patience and waited for her to get up from the new sleep she had gone into.

"Oh, this is magical!" she exclaimed as she lifted her head and looked at me as if she had fallen into a magical spell.

"What happened?" I asked with utter surprise.

"I sensed something, a feeling I have been through long years ago; I am marvelled by how the feeling reverberated, taking me back to my dream of twenty years ago," she said with a sense of fulfilment that had burgeoned in due course as she expressed everything about Shivani to me.

"But Khuda why did you ask me to do this?"

"I simply wanted you to listen to Mother Earth"

"Mother Earth!" she exclaimed.

"You seemed to want to know more about all those thoughts that have been lingering on your mind. So I felt if Mother Earth has been listening to your mind for so long, she may have something to convey if you listened," I replied.

"Yes, it is so true. I felt as if someone was instructing me to understand more about the vision I had witnessed. I also felt as if somebody was inviting me into a conversation about Shivani."

"It was none else but Mother Earth who was talking. As one prostrates and touches the forehead at her feet she rushes into the arena of that person immediately and attends to understand the thoughts."

"What do you mean by arena?" she asked.

"It is the space of seven palms around you, the measurement of a royal cubit, within which floats your aura and the energies, it is your energies that convey your state of mind to her." I said

She looked amazed at this novel aspect.

"You mean to say that the spirit we talk about and the energies that we get from the universe actually come from Mother Earth? It really must be the case because it is said in the scriptures too that we are made up of earth, this very mud that we walk on and after our death we go back to her."

I opened the *Ketaab-e-Hayaat* and went to Page 151, it read:

> *They both were walking to a village seven miles away from Jerusalem. Christ had already been crucified. On the way they meet a stranger who talks to them about the richness and the truth hidden in the scriptures. They continue to walk with the stranger for seven miles, listening to him and discussing about what had just happened in Jerusalem. They decide to eat together and find the stranger breaking the bread for them; their eyes suddenly brighten as they find that the stranger is none other than the resurrected Christ.*

I lifted my eyes and gazed at my own past; Zeba too had told me about crossing many destinations, to reach the seventh one. Was she referring to my seven-mile journey? Was Christ accompanying me as well? Zeba definitely was. The journey with her for the first 14 years had made me realize much more than the scriptures could.

The next day I narrated the story of seven miles to Satviki, and she suddenly reacted to it.

"Are you planning to resume your journey? Is that why you are telling me this story?"

I felt the jolt and awakened to the fact that I was very much on my journey, I had not forgotten about it but an urge to wait for Shivani had kind of postponed my thoughts about it.

"Yes, of course, I do plan to move ahead and reach the destination I had planned for."

"And what about resurrected Christ who should accompany you to Fatehpur?" she smiled and asked me about my plans.

"Spending seven weeks with you all in total silence were perhaps those seven miles of my entire life," I said.

34

I was no more a stranger to both of them. They often shared their concerns about Shivani either together or sometimes one by one to me. He being a father often ended with weary eyes when he talked about his only fortune and joy. Sometimes he even shared with me things related to the tradition of bidding goodbye to a daughter after her marriage, and mentioned about her seventh lord being in the seventh house. I could never understand these equations. But looking at one's horoscope was a common practice in this part of the world. A lot was determined for a child as soon as he or she was born. I was reminded of the *fal-namas* that people referred to back in Hamadan. Knowing one's future was one idea I could not relate to and so understanding my own fate through some external aspects was unacceptable.

For a moment I closed my eyes and had a flash of vision.

"As long as I live, I want to be your nurse, your companion, I want to read to you, walk with you, and be your eyes and hands to you," I found myself telling her.

It was the realization of the dream of finding true love. I had once read in the *Ketaab-e-Hayaat* that you often see the shadow of the person you are in love with in your dreams well before you see the person actually. Perhaps, this dream had returned to me many times and I actually saw the shadow transforming into an image and soon the image into a person standing in front of me.

I was strengthened by her powers, I had become vocal with her voice, I had been gifted a free will by the silent messiah.

I became still, my eyes turned motionless, and my soul overwhelmed. I felt as if I was under some magical spell. Her incessant thoughts had made me rise in gratitude to the lord almighty and to her parents who were none other but a reflection of that same spirit I was longing to meet.

⟶◆⟵

My destiny was calling me as ever. I asked both of them to allow me to take their leave to fulfil what god had wished for me . . . .

"What is this?"

"*Gayatri*, the prayer that brings the seven rays that emanate from the sun, the creator and the protector of our lives, the one who shines with seven rays, the one who assumes the forms of time and illumines all, the generator of light in our lives."

"How do I carry this paper, shall I keep it in this book?" I asked Satviki.

"You could either put it in your book, or roll it and enclose it into a talisman," she said.

"Like this?" I rolled up my sleeve and showed her the one that was tied on my arm.

"Yes," she said with a surprise.

Little did she know that the talisman also had another *Gayatri* in it, the 'Haft Mobin' that was meant to save me from all evils. If only I had told her about it, she would have immediately connected it to saving of my life from the thieves and my reaching the umbrella of her motherhood.

Benazir Patil

I looked at the *Gayatri* and closed my eyes, I suddenly felt as if I was soaring high, already reaching heights like the birds in search of my *Simorgh*.

"Never feel alone and afraid of anything, soar like an eagle, and bless the world with your niceness. You had all the patience and humility in the adversity you faced. The bravery in you personifies the goodness god wanted in each one of us. For us you are just like Shivani, the strength of our life, the inspiration to do good when tribulations knocked our door. Come back to us whenever you feel like, there will be a time when we will be happy to be nursed by you."

My path had not changed either, but something had transformed, a rising sun and the illuminating moon looked like blessings I had never felt before. Everything around existed as it was, but looked rejuvenated to me, perhaps the idiosyncrasies of my youth were flourishing at their own pace. Sometimes I conversed with Zeba and sometimes with Daniyaal but it was all about Shivani. Talking about her was sheer happiness.

Men come on earth to refresh the example of the highest ideals of human life, and to reawaken mankind to the possibility of establishing internal connections with God, the Divine Beloved in every heart. My recent life had become my whole world; and more than the world: almost my hope of heaven. She stood between me and every thought of my psyche, as an eclipse intervenes between the moon and the broad sun. I could not, in those days, see through or think of the almighty either.

The thought of Fatehpur continued as ever but a voice within beckoned I were to come back here very soon.

35

I sat at the tea stall, watching and observing the cries of the street vendors, a pale-faced sixteen-year-old boy was serving tea to the regular pilgrims coming to the shrine— he reminded me of myself at that age while I worked in the merchant's yard in Yazd. My keen observation of him resulted in a sudden meeting of our eyes, I extended a quiet smile; he took some time, but smiled back. It seemed as if his smile had travelled from one of the deepest corners of his heart and very slowly reached his eyes. It wasn't bare; it carried some tears along. A thirst aroused in me, to reach out to him. However, for the next two days we both conversed in silence, neither of us had felt like strangers, the connectivity was rather ancient.

On the third day I decided to buy some tea from him but found that he was nowhere to be seen. I earnestly enquired, and found that his mother's illness had called for his presence in his nearby village. The teapot and a couple of cups were the only asset he possessed. The worry was not so much about his homelessness as much as his loneliness that I had seen in his eyes. I thought of him continuously, he was so much like me.

After my arrival in Amritsar I had regaled this assumption that I was longing to go back. I had spent the previous night continuously thinking about the wavered feelings in my mind and had gone straight to bed in a small attic in which I had put myself up. The following morning I discovered a singular fascination for the time I had spent in Gujranwala. And somehow, there was a general sense of niceness every time I reminisced those moments.

Jayant and I breakfasted at eight in the morning and then he took me to the mill where I was to get a job that would fetch me daily wages. While the mill supervisor took his mug of tea and hunch of bread, he looked at me from top to bottom and demanded a quiet reassurance from Jayant about me. I considered him to be doing this with every employee who would be approaching him. The mill-man's conversation consisted of nothing but some calculations with Jayant, which I was unaware of.

On my politely asking him about what next, he said, pompously, "Start, right away, come with me, it will take two days for you to learn the job, but I guess you will need to keep your energy levels intact to deliver skillfully."

How could I have answered, in a strange place, with no knowledge of what I was to do, I went ahead with him. Till date I had worked in numerous places, I had maintained stocks in the warehouse in Yazd, worked as a nurse for Shamsher in Bamiyan, managed a large business for Mir Raza, had been a learner in Gujranwala, and sometimes I had even ended up doing odd jobs that I needed to keep myself going with the meager demands of worldly life. For such reasons, I was very glad that I was going to work here and earn some more for my onward journey.

I could see that everyone around me was seeking happiness, but very few had achieved it, for lasting happiness dawns only when there is complete freedom from wants. This highest state of non-wanting may seem outwardly to imply inaction and to be easy of attainment. However, if anyone tries to sit quietly without inwardly wanting anything and with full consciousness (that is, without going to sleep), he will realize that such a state of non-wanting is very difficult to attain and that it can be sustained only through tremendous spiritual activity. In fact, complete non-wanting is unattainable as long as life is mind-ridden. It is possible only in supra-mental existence. One has to go beyond the mind to experience the spiritual bliss of desire-less-ness.

Jayant seemed to be lonely. I did not ask him much but he soon shared with me, he had lost his wife while delivering their child, the misery had magnified as the child also did not survive, he was someone who could not feel the grace of almighty.

Life and love seemed inseparable to him

"My love for Janaki was the driving power to reach that spiritual entity but after having lost her, I often think if that entity really exists, and if it does what the hell am I being punished for? But somehow I feel He does not exist."

Jayant had reached a stage of complete confusion about his existence; he found it difficult to understand what he was to live with, and what he would do without his companion who he had promised to live through his seven births. However, he had lost her in this very birth. As love gathers strength it also generates restlessness. I did think of asking him more about his state of mind but felt that it would be better to let him share by himself . . .

I was reminded of Shah Baba's words, "Stop running away from the reality and do not hate any aspect of your life for a moment. Do not deny the actions of the self or of the almighty. Look at those pains within you, understand what they are meant for, just as happiness contributes to the growth of your entire being so does pain."

Benazir Patil

The reality stood in front of me. People who ardently visited temples also traded in religion. People who glorified the lord uttered glorifying lies with the same tongue. People who took pride in their strength oppressed the weak. People who talked about peace extended cruelties to others. People who rejoiced in the name of the almighty crushed the happiness and became tyrants to their slaves.

———※———

One day at daybreak I sat at the shrine listening to the chanting. No knowledge of language was required to understand the praise of god. An old man with a long beard continued to observe my intense involvement.

"How have you managed to reach this stage of detachment at such a young age?" he questioned me as I opened my eyes and gazed at his observance of me.

Meditation and listening to the enchantments had pushed me into a state of trance; I understood his question but felt a little lost in finding an answer. I remained quiet for some time, but soon realized that my silence would offend him.

As I was preparing myself to respond to him, he spoke again, "Our existence can really be futile, isn't it? Though a thought like this can seem miserable, it is indeed real. Because, we are not born with any predefined aims or connotations about our life, the meaning evolves as we decide how we should lead it, so the aims can never come from outside, it has to come from within."

His expression of life's aim and purpose had triggered my senses; I was all set to tell him what I felt about it.

"I agree, there was a time when I would question others about the purpose of my existence, but the question does not exist anymore, that I am alive, I exist to complete some unfinished task I have been assigned to, the soul inside directs me to it, and I can sense the depth of my reality in this universe," I responded.

The pleasantness on his face indicated that he had liked my answer and felt the urge to converse more.

"Is it not difficult to explain the bliss of detachment to someone who is attached to things and places? How does one tell him what freedom really means when he is imprisoned by the extravagance around him?" he asked me.

"An urge to break free from attachments and desires also comes from within; it is inexplicable, a walk from material confinement to spiritual freedom is nothing but a self-inspired experience. So neither of us can or needs to explain anything to anyone." I responded with a smile as I had gauged the mischief in his eyes as he put forth the question, three times my age had made him treat me like a young child.

My instant response made him laugh heartily, "Do you come here often?" he asked me.

"Yes, almost every day, mostly at day break."

"So do I, surely, we will meet again," he said taking my leave.

I aspired to meet him again, not for learning anything, but to experience the contentment and ease he carried with him, the abundance his empty hands possessed.

Benazir Patil

I came home and opened the *Ketaab-e-Hayaat,* Page 61, it read:

> *The seventh part of Jap Ji says, despite all the fame, one will not be recognized unless one has god's grace, god confers virtues on the non-virtuous and more virtues on the pious.*

> *Verse 1: Even if you lived the four ages, or even ten times more*

> *Verse 2: and even if you were known throughout the nine continents and everyone followed you,*

> *Verse 3: With a good name and reputation, the whole world sang your praises*

> *Verse 4: Still, if you do not please the Lord, no one will ask about you!*

> *Verse 5: Among worms, you would be considered a lowly worm, and even contemptible sinners would hold you in contempt.*

> *Verse 6: O Nanak, He makes unworthy worthy and gives virtues to the virtuous.*

> *Verse 7: I know of no other who can grant so much to others!*

From the following day onwards the human inside me looked for him every time I entered the shrine, but I could not find him. We had not exchanged our names either, but it had been so since my childhood, I always met the person I longed to meet eagerly. I often wondered if this was something exceptional to me; however, with my connection with Mother Earth I had found that she responded to all my intentions; when I really longed to meet someone or understand something, she gave an understanding ear and fulfilled my aspirations. My miniscule energies were always reinforced by her abundant energies; she made me feel so powerful that sometimes my soul could converse with Zeba by entering her timeless universe. Whether it was meeting Shivani or the old man in the shrine, it definitely was not serendipitous. They were equally a part of my unfinished tasks, the purpose for which I existed.

The question of understanding the purpose of one's life was not merely a question one could raise; it was connected to comprehension of the divine, a knowledge that gradually crept into our lives only through our consciousness, a consciousness that created inspiration to understand the self, a self that threw light on the occurrences of our life and the intentions of our mind, the intentions that encouraged actions, the actions that gave us learning, the learning that helped us in discernment and harmonized our body and the soul, the soul that inspired selflessness, the selflessness that led to detachment and the detachment that enlightened us with an eternal peace. The search of understanding our purpose culminated in finding everlasting harmony. The unfinished task when completed led us to a path of enlightenment.

My thoughts wandered in the midst of the glory that was slowly spreading around the shrine, I suddenly sensed a familiar hand patting my back.

"You had been waiting to meet me," the old man said.

"Ah yes, I thought of you every day, wondered where you had gone," I responded.

"Nowhere, I was busy in some unfinished tasks," he smiled and said.

"So does life seem perfect now?" I smiled back and asked.

"It always was."

"And how do you say that with complete assurance."

"Because, it's a complete surrender to the almighty, there is nothing that I long for and nothing that I regret having lost."

Though I knew that the saints were singing praises of god, I asked him what it meant:

"'*Jap*' means meditation on an object to a degree that one loses his consciousness and merges into the very object of meditation. The meditation turns the meditator into that very object, losing all sense of his own separate existence, to the extent that it effaces the tint of ego in man, letting in Divinity, which already exists in him with full expressive effulgence. '*Ji*' means a new life achieved through meditation, which brings us in closer communion with the Ever-Existent source of life. Thus '*Jap Ji*' contains within itself the solutions to the mystery of life," he responded and continued.

"And do you know that each *pauri* of the '*Jap Ji*' has its role in human life?" he asked.

"*Pauri*?" I expressed my negligence

"*Pauri*, literally means a ladder to walk up, is a stanza that all of us recite."

"And what role does it play?" I asked.

"It is like when you suffer from greed, madness for power, when you become trapped in your territoriality, it is the reciting of the seventh *pauri* that actually heals you."

Benazir Patil

All human actions have one or more of these seven causes: chance, nature, compulsions, habit, reason, passion and desire.

Aristotle

36

"There was not an idle moment from dawn to dusk. We both sat in the veranda and looked at the distant lands, which were the only boundaries that we could envision. With no flashes of interest and desire, even our eyes had refused to converse with each other. It was a hard battle fought minute by minute; not like chasing a conquest, but more like struggling in the whirlwind. Warped up in our own environs where we had lived for years, we stared in silence through the window and over the darkened shadows, now and then our minds patted each other with a blurred hope," he narrated listlessly with longer pauses.

"Was it a foolish trick of chance that had dragged us to this situation? Who was instrumental for all that none of us could fathom in so many years? Twenty of us belonged to the unwanted community; our children grew up learning the lessons of love and giving, but suddenly the display of cruelty in those tragic moments had caused them disbelief in the entire humanity. In the heart of our hearts, we were sure about the protection our friends would extend, those with whom we had shared pleasures and tears, but that was only a hope perhaps," he said.

I was the first listener Khushaal Singh had met with after all the havoc he and his family had been through. My expressions conveyed him the urge to know more about those tragic moments.

"Suddenly everything had become empty. On that day we knew we could never live happily like before, the spring of our brotherhood was vanishing. Each instance was becoming abominable as we started hearing of voices we were waiting for the whole day," he continued with a dazed stare.

"No wonder, Shivani had heard the first uproar coming from far, she had made us aware, her mind was always on guard against dangers; she was born with some instinctive powers. It was a faint sound initially, and in no time we heard people breathing at our front door. With a feeling of terror, we turned to each other. But by the time we could ensure safety, some five terror-struck men barged into our house without a tinge of fear or intentions of conversation. They had gotten to know from somewhere that we had gathered at one place to protect each other from the unthinkable devastation that was approaching us, lest, to die with each other. The news of houses getting burnt one after the other in other towns had been spreading since a day or two. Men beating drums and shouting boisterously was a scene that was described to us, but none of us could hold that belief. Because, everybody around were our people, no strangers resided along the town," he said.

"What happened after they entered your home?" I asked eagerly

"They pushed us with disgrace and held some of us tightly, so that we could not move or protect our families. After checking the possessions and riches stored in trunks, they poured oil all around our houses and set the fire. The smell and sound of flames swept us completely, but the mind was continuously consoling that we may get spared. Shivani, one of the youngest amongst us was the most matured."

"I saw Shivani pushing herself and Satviki out of fire. It seemed as if she was vacillating between the two temptations, whether to run away from that dreadful thing or to jump into it. She could see the fire of hatred rising all around her.

I could see her expressions from a distance, neither of anger, nor of hatred, they were those of listening to the inkling; she stood there in a state of calmness, waiting for the command from the almighty. As she stood there, unperturbed, I saw a man pushing her aside from the fire; I could not recognize him, for I had never seen him before. I was aghast at myself, ashamed too, I could not reach her or Satviki, and I was struggling to unwind myself from a blaze that had suddenly entangled me in its aura. The houses were falling apart, the flames were getting exhausted. The light of the day had come to an end, the darkness stood illuminated with man-made light of horrors. Some of us managed to come together, but we could react to nothing, we had no choice but to wait till day break, to find out more about the lost souls."

"Were you able to trace Shivani later?" I questioned him desperately.

"I had witnessed Shivani being saved, but I was restless throughout the night as a thousand thoughts rushed through my mind when I questioned myself about the identity of the man I had seen: he was a middle-aged man, from behind he resembled like Uncle Jalal who stayed behind in their house, but I soon lost their sight in the sparkling flames. I was unsure of what I was thinking; I had no other option but control my unbridled thoughts, leading me into a suffering I was sinking into," he responded.

"Was that the last sight of Shivani that you had?"

"My eyes stood completely open all night. In the wake hours of morning, I again saw a hazy picture of a limping man carrying a half-dead girl on his shoulders. I stood up to reach him to gather who he was carrying, but by the time I could walk up to him he had disappeared, my old eyes felt cheated and my heart questioned my brain if I was hallucinating." he added.

The 7th Destination

Those few weeks of blessed exile, I had stolen glimpses of Shivani from wherever I could. Every time I saw her serene face, I had felt as if all the brilliance of nature had contributed to her creation and only the unworthy souls were incapable of understanding her charisma. Every time I heard her discussing passionately about someone's pain, I could hear god declaring delightfully, "Listen mankind, be the onlookers of my elegance, my brightness, my purity and my virtue". My mind oscillated back and forth as I stood in front of the old man who still debated with himself about her existence.

"Wonder what had happened to all of us, we had always lived harmonious lives without any ill feelings, in absolute bliss of friendliness, fervour and passion, so often me and my other friends hopped on to lorries to go to fairs and festivals to each other's town, but that day, all of them had come on horses, with a difficult intention, armed with knives and swords. Those attacks seemed endless, I had read about wars in my books, but had not contemplated it as something that meant attacking the unwary and the innocents. The killings were merciless, a surge to fight back appeared every now and then but the morale was collapsing as rapidly as the flames were infringing us, even the young children were not spared, growing fears in women had led them to the brink of wells, the wells that had fetched them with life all these years had become the custodians of their dead bodies." He paused and continued to explain, my heart was quivering with an imagination of the ghastly picture that appeared out of his narrative.

"Men and women were flocking and running away, I had no clue where they wanted to run away, to a safe refuge perhaps, ironically, they were searching for a refuge which they could not find in their own homes. I could not fathom this plight, I stood in my home, I could not think of a home outside mine, I could not think searching for refuge in the world that was unknown

Benazir Patil

to me," he said and sat quietly for some time without uttering a word. Something had overwhelmed him, some thoughts that had arrested his speech. I refrained from interrogating any further; I stood up and took his hands in mine.

"Days and nights have come and gone, I have been waiting to hear about my sister and my daughter who I never saw after that fateful night," he almost broke down as he shared his plight.

Suddenly I heard someone calling my name.

The optimism had not ended! Even a call from someone awakened me to the feeling of oneness with her; I felt as if someone would walk in with her and say, "Here is Shivani!"

"They were instilling fright for life in us and all of us were willingly harvesting the crop of terror laden with fruits of brutality. When they told me to leave my world and search for peace elsewhere, I had no clue what they were talking about," he continued.

He kept sketching the composition of killings. I could understand where he was coming from. He was convinced that the indulging businessmen who wanted to loot humanity of its faith were engineering conflicts. He had not ventured upon a journey of uncertainties, but his staying back home had not left him in peace either, the loss of his dear ones in front of his eyes had made him feel like a victim of his own decision.

I wondered how the soul must have evolved in human beings, and if it were a part of every human being. Then, what had gone wrong with some of those that Khushaal Singh was talking about. It is the soul alone which has made humans believe that they had a life even after death and that they never could become immortal without a soul.

37

The mind had its ebb and flow of unrest, with peace creeping in slowly at times, receding its steps unknowingly. I was back to the town of the holy shrine, wondering how long I would take to accept the truth about Shivani's departure to the holy abode of the lord. Though Khushaal Singh had shared about his loneliness in his own so-called home and motherland, I was not sure what it meant; I had resided in nature's bounties, alien lands and among unknown people, and at every place I felt as if I had always known that part of the world. I asked myself if I wanted to believe what Khushaal Singh had narrated, his perceptions could have been either an accident or a mistake.

At a loss for action, I continued sitting in the shrine, gazing from one man to another. Khushaal Singh had unburdened his mind by telling me the truth he believed in, many women on that dreadful night had done away with the humiliation they were likely to face by jumping into the wells and he was sure that Shivani was also one of them—he had seen the heap of limbs that were piled in the well near his house.

While he shared with me the most awful details of the event, some parts of his mind still lay hidden, completely hidden from the shattered world. It was miraculous to see him with an obsession of generating love in the midst of all the tragedy he was going through.

For ten consecutive days in the midst of misery around me, I could hardly sleep for a few hours in the night. God perhaps had a complex plan of pacifying him by my presence in his vicinity for those ten days. In the eyes of the world, I was the only one in Gujranwala whose family member had not suffered with any misery, but my misery was irreparable and could not be expressed in words. Little did Khushaal Singh know about me while I had stayed at the prayer-man's house, but in these days he had understood my loss, he had realized what it was for me to lose Shivani and her family. After three days of sharing his loss, he had stopped talking about it, he could just perceive those tears in my eyes which I could not roll down; this was the second time in my life when misery was beyond my apprehension and control. At the time of Zeba's death I could rightfully cry but in those ten days I could not; a social inhibition had taken over me and numbness of my eyes was the only outlet.

I religiously visited every nook and corner of the town with an estimated optimism. My eyes failed to notice all the others that lived in the town. Finding someone from Shivani's family was impractical. If we all did what we decided, as devotedly as I was doing, we would end up living in a place akin to paradise, I thought to myself. After many years in life, I had found myself doing nothing else, not that I had been a great entrepreneur in the past but I definitely was working enough to earn for my living. Though Khushaal Singh had told me not to approach the police, as he had not been able to find much information from them, I kept going and meeting them every afternoon for my own consolation.

In the midst of the misery, I turned to the *Ketaab-e-Hayaat*, only to open Page 214, it read:

Sūrat al-Takwīr, the Seventh in the chronology of revelation discloses the signs of the coming of the day of judgment.

When the sun will be folded up;

When the stars will swoop down;

When the mountains will be set in motion;

When the pregnant she-camels will be abandoned;

When the wild beasts will be gathered together;

When the seas will be flared up;

When the people will be arranged in categories;

When the girl-child that was buried alive will be asked, for what sin she was killed;

When the scrolls (of deeds) will be unrolled;

When the sky will be stripped off;

When the Hell will be set ablaze;

And when the Paradise will be brought close.

Motionless, I stood there, for a moment I felt small, like a small animal who could be hunted by its fellow animals of the same species. For the first and only time I sensed that I was completely alone. Since the day of Zeba's death I had made many relationships of the world that stood like cherished pages of a book, which I went back to and read when I felt like. With Shivani, there was no relation of the world, it was a connection of my spirit, my mind had not been able to move to another page, it seemed to me as though her page had become the last and concluding page of my book; I could not and had not gathered the strength to come to another worldly connection. Years together I had lived without a home of my own, because I did not need one, for me the universe was a given home from the almighty, I was to share it with everyone, so neither could contemplate

Benazir Patil

of owning nor disowning it. Even in my deepest meditation I had never felt alone and homeless under the mammoth umbrella of *Al-Kabeer*, the greatest of all.

I had not been anybody other than Khudabakhsh, I inhaled and exhaled the love that god showered on me. I needed no refuge, no relationships, no caretakers, yet I could love the people I met, I could look after them, and I could be their solace.

Neither had I dwelled in the forest with the hermits, nor had I joined the procession that struggled to spread the word of gods. In Shivani, I had been able to meet with the contemporary saint. I wanted to follow her on her path.

Just when I had entered this bliss, I saw that my world was melting away, as if god had aimed to give me the final lesson on detachment, he wanted to shake me up and tell me the truth of my life that I was not sent to the world to get attached to people. If my love and longing for Shivani was spiritual what was I brooding over, why did I want to see her image, was her impression in my mind not sufficient for me to adore her and live by every word she had gifted me with?

She had given the most to my evolution and I was perhaps insulting her by crying over her absence. She gave me the lessons on the reality of birth and death, she taught me those seven arts of living life. In those three months I had lived years, as every moment spent with her left memories that enriched several years of my life.

I shook myself off that flitting thought: how could I ever be alone after having met the model of god on earth? How could I fool myself so easily and revert to the worldly saga? I felt suddenly surrounded by a strange aura, my nerves environed with energy, a divine voice told me I had lost nothing, I was asked to walk out of the worldly realm and enter the spiritual where death only meant an exit to enter a new beginning. With wide open eyes I looked around and found no one, I could only gather the truth after closing my eyes, only to realize that the voice came from within.

The *parwaaz*, the onset of my journey after Zeba's death, had guided me through the inroads of human consciousness. This was another one perhaps, I was once again told to soar high and fly through the clouds of unknown. Slowly I was to rise above the world and look at it from a distance, to realize that one day I would go back to the earth and the skies with just my soul and nothing else.

Five days passed, and the sky was still heavy with dark clouds. I made three attempts to leave but something kept stopping me. Khushaal Singh continued to give me kind glances and pleaded that there was enough daily bread for the two of us. He said that he could see the light in me, and that would help him see the light in others, the events of the past few days had blinded him of the brightness of humanity. He feared and wondered about his brothers next door.

On the tenth day, I decided to move on and journey on to Fatehpur.

Khushaal Singh believed that in the circumstances that were all in and the havoc people were passing through, with untold miseries, it was best for me not to languish in Gujranwala with false hopes but to accept the reality and move on. Words cannot narrate the sense I had at that moment. No loss in my life had ever pushed me into this kind of mournfulness. It was a strange feeling of having lost someone whom I had admired only silently. This feeling had put me into a state of indescribable awe about myself.

Benazir Patil

Despite knowing that no one lived there anymore, I went to the prayer-man's house once again for the last time. I looked into the room where I had last seen her before I left for Amritsar, and I imagined her seated on the divan near the hearth with her back towards the garden. In the instant when I was retreating myself to leave peacefully, I sensed a bizarre feeling of seeing her walking out of the flames towards me. I was amazed at my intensity of thoughts on her. It was like an awakening. I was seized by a vehement confidence about getting engaged in an earth-shattering conversation with her—I was so close yet so far from the bare truth!

38

It is the mind that creates the thoughts; a thought is heralded by some kind of form in the mind. I was also creating something in my mind without much realization. I was not aware what form and structures I was creating. But, I always had this minute inkling about what was to occur in my life next, not that there were no surprises; the inkling only made me conscious to something untoward or favourable about to happen. It was much later that I had found in the *Ketaab-e-Hayaat* that our own thoughts preceded beliefs and beliefs preceded occurrences.

So little did I understand of myself until I found that our own thoughts were responsible for our realities! These thoughts had a definite purpose, sometimes they were like a quietly flowing river with utmost discipline and direction and sometimes they were just like whirlwinds where I could guess its two distinct ends. This was not all, there was another concurrent process, hitting of other peoples' thoughts on the walls of my mind; some I received and some I let go—did not want them to assimilate with mine. This is what I had continuously experienced when I lived in the prayer-man's house; Shivani's thoughts kept thumping my mind like rigorous waves of the ocean. Her gestures were simple, I was absolutely overpowered by two things: one was my fate, the loss of knowing myself; the other was a blessing, her speech.

Rarely do we perceive the simplicity of our minds in realizing who we are and where we want to go, perhaps we take it for granted this is something that we are born with.

Sunshine had begun to desert my small room, early evening was inviting the twilight which seemed a bit dreary. With sinking courage and a forlorn mood I was unable to make any decisions, but I had to. How long could I wait to get those inklings that I had lived by for so many years? All said, I was dejected inside with a loss which I had never anticipated as one. Had it not been for those riots I would have rarely gone back in search of Shivani. Why was I wanting myself to meet her again? was it only because of my fear of her death? or I had promised myself to meet her again in this very lifetime? I had never been so unsure of my own thoughts. I wished I could go back to that well and bring her out myself and be her limbs, her speech, her life and her breath.

"Living and loving are two inseparable aspects of every life," I had once heard Shivani telling this to Sadhana her childhood friend. "Every living being has been blessed with this binding consciousness of loving another life form."

"But I don't really know if love can ever be true?" Sadhana had questioned.

"Love can only be true. If it is not true, it cannot be love; the only emotion that bonds you into a feeling of oneness; an expression that cheers you up and refills your quintessence with contradictions of greed; an arena that does not ask you to confine yourself to; an only possession that does not let you accumulate but give," responded Shivani.

"This sounds so much like the impressions spelt out in books, how this can be true and occurring?" she questioned again.

"The concepts and impressions that you read in books are nothing but emotions spelt out by human mind. Exclusion of love from our lives may almost mean the cessation of our soul from our bodies. Love is strength, the energy and the power that drives our entire consciousness."

A remarkable impression dawned upon me. I marvelled, had she been alive, how she would have reacted to my coming over in search of her.

I looked at the burnt bed, blackened walls, turned my eyes intermittently towards the darkened sky, I recalled the prayer-man's very first mention about his daughter with me.

The prayer-man often touched my forehead with his palms and tried to feel something about me—I never understood much about it. But one day he sensed the curiosity in my eyes and said, "I am examining the chakras in your body."

"Shivani not only can explain about the seven chakras in our bodies, but she also has a theory for the seven senses: she says that a soul of man is influenced by seven different elements in the universe."

My stay with Khushaal Singh revealed a lot about the human inside me, I realized that the understanding we achieve from the sensitivity for those walking through an ordeal may not fetch us much clarity about their state of mind; by all means it does let us amalgamate our identity with theirs, sometimes it is so perceptible that their miseries and their joys become our own.

It is indeed difficult for anyone to decide what one will do until one faces the trial. I was not sure if I had ever been prepared to deal with an emergency like that one. A man as him and so many other men had devoted all their lives in looking after their families—that would have included their efforts in providing security too—but a peril so unwanted and uncalled for had brought them to a standstill. Everything

Benazir Patil

was over for many of them. There was neither anything to look back nor to look forward to. Peace and harmony had now become burdens they could not carry, because there was nothing they could restore with all of those principles. Strangely, it had made humanity question the intentions of God: were these means of shaping out His enigmatic intentions justified? Were these His ways of challenging people's faiths? Was this His scheme to unveil the obscure shrouds that hid the faces of evil?

I was reminded of Zeba; to most people she said that God is just an assumption, not a truth, a judgment based on some verifications whose adequacy is never questioned, an entity that exists out of this universe, and does not portray any personal connection while they are sinning. The goodness is meant to be exercised only by Him and not by His subjects. His subjects are meant to be forgiven for all the sins they did.

Khushaal Singh guided me not to go alone, so I joined a group of people who were moving towards Amritsar. I was confused; had I come here only as a mere spectator to go back empty-handed, with no power to challenge my destiny?

39

It had been one of the rarest mornings of my life when I was unable to get out of bed despite being soaked by the bright light of the day. I sat wrapped in a shawl, felt weak in the flesh and broken mentally—there cannot be a worse ailment than an indescribable dejection of mind, a misery that kept generating quiet tears. Yet, I thought I should have been thankful to god for having given me a taste of a feeling called love which I would not have otherwise realized ever. My state of mind had always known so much bliss, comfortable as I was to an existence of perpetual contentment and satisfying discrimination; my tired anxiety was then in a condition that no peace could relieve me of the dejection I was experiencing.

But, happily for me there was a counterbalance now, by the fact that my love for her was infinitely more powerful than anything that I was experiencing around me, and by my will alone I could carry all my mental vibrations to her.

Death, however, could not be ignored; it extracted generous revenge from within. Phases of life and death can be equated to the swapping intervals of sleep and awareness. Sleep organizes us for the coming day's doings; so does death for the next life perhaps.

I prostrated and listened to Mother Earth.

"Human spirit is more than just a life force, your will, your conscience and your understanding is a part of the spirit that resides within you. There are conditions of misery and ecstasy that the spirit will encounter from time to time, it is more becoming to trust in god, He is author of all forms, so be it, He is the only one who will tell the truth of your life to you."

I got up and thought about the message that Mother Earth had transmitted. She was true, god had poured a lot of reasoning into my mind but then the impulse existed as well.

My disillusioned analysis of human bondage had brought me on the brink of being an unbeliever. I, in my despair, was incapable of enduring reality! my despair was no illustration of personal weakness; those were essential moments required for the progress of my innateness.

Pleasure, being the root of every man; he is rarely happy about what he achieves. The world of misery is more perceptible than that of happiness. Having lived with a small bag consisting of three pairs of long shirts, ankle length pyjamas, two hand woven caps and a small pouch with meagre cash for my survival I had not pondered much about what could be more pleasurable than an existence like mine.

Incidentally, the small pouch also had a small ring from Zeba with a slightly large emerald affixed on it. I had no clue why Zeba had given it to me, in my childhood I had heard of stories of kings and queens handing over their most precious possessions to the princes and princesses in their last moments.

40

The evening was as feverish as I was. I thought of going to bed, but the dismal interiors disallowed my restless soul to rest. I looked around for water. My mind was reminded of drinking some water, which I had refrained from throughout the day, wondered if I had lost thirst as well. Despite the inclination, I left it untouched. Perhaps, the matter-of-fact things had become too distant to me. Strangely, there was water outside too; it had rained badly after many days. Someone in the neighborhood had expressed it as a boon in the times of countless curses. I was as involved in everything around me as I was in myself, isolation never came naturally to me, I could never manage to cut a miserable figure of myself, neither could I recall if misery had ever crossed me in last so many years.

After the rain stopped I walked about eight miles to reach someone I had planned to meet. The whole day I missed Amritsar, so often had I moved from one city to another, with occasional memories, but Amritsar was different, wondered what had attracted me to it: was it the people, the welcoming sorts or was it the shrine that had triggered my journey to Fatehpur again. Something in that place had changed me again and had brought me back to life.

I had heard in my childhood, a place becomes holy by the deposits of spiritual vibrations left by prophets and saints who lived or visited there. Pilgrimage to a holy place becomes rewarding spiritually when the pilgrim is able to transport himself to the historical time of the prophets and saints associated with the holy place and, inspired by spiritual longing, is able to reflect upon and commune with their lives and actions, witness through his eyes of devotion the events that happened there, and bathe himself in the holy memories of the place. For a person devoid of spiritual longing and devotion, a mere visit to a holy place does not become a pilgrimage.

While returning home, I had happened to enter into a conversation with a middle-aged man at a roadside tea-shop. Presuming he belonged to Delhi, I was keen to get some information from him. But, the Sikh with a light orange turban and a stylish beard revealed that he was new to Delhi, had travelled from Lahore just a few months ago and was more knowledgeable about the similarities and dissimilarities between Lahore and Amritsar. As we sipped some tea and turned a little more sociable, our acquaintance cornered my reason for being there. He had been kind enough to ask me a number of indirect questions, with an only urge to know if I was from the North West Frontier Province. His limited assumption of me had emanated from his need to know the whereabouts of his childhood friend who had lived there. The truth about me had brought sadness in his eyes. The pain of his ignorance was much revealing.

Loads and loads of people had travelled to Delhi after the inhuman havoc; had the prayer-man been alive, even he would have migrated to this city perhaps as he would have to walk the path towards this side of the world I thought.

✦

I walked and walked, being sentient, that there was no going back. My journey to Zeba's birthplace had resumed, out of many purposes that I had fulfilled, the one to reach there stood in front of me as ever. Life, in many possible ways, was still teaching me the techniques to reunite with reality. Still alive and filled with energy, I wanted to understand

The 7th Destination

the reason of the so-destined purpose of going to Fatehpur. The happenings in the last few months had reassured me compellingly that Zeba did not want me to go there for nothing. The manifestations of her one wish had made me cross several lives in just one. There had been times when I was aloof, other times when I was deeply involved in understanding the material world, times when I was sick of all of that, moments when I had reincarnated into a stronger me, and there were spells when I got immersed into deep emotions. The reality of disease, misery and loss could only be slain by the sentiments that I held within. Had it not been for Zeba, I would have lived in Hamadan forever, and walked on the other side of the world as a *dervish*. As a child I knew that not many people had travelled to the lands of cold seas.

Unquestionably, my existence had been delightful; the odd and even tracks that I walked on were as much a part of my life as everyone else's. Yet, the distractions that were considered distractions by others were not really distractions for me: my upbringing by a solitary but strong woman; an inherent inquisitiveness about the *Ketaab-e-Hayaat*; the unplanned *parwaaz* at the age of fourteen; experiencing the depth of meditation with Shah Baba; excelling in business with Mir Raza; understanding the magnificence of 'Om' from the prayer-man; and losing Shivani even before my thoughts could reach her psyche, were not merely co-incidences, each one of it was connected to something or the other. Either the effects had causes or the causes had effects.

I meditated, the aspiring music of nature entered into my being, it was bringing all the healing energies, creating a balance and harmony in all that was being planned in my mind. The vices of impatience, anger and suspicion had disappeared. All the seven rays of the sun were orchestrating their influence on my consciousness.

Benazir Patil

An aspiration rested in my mind, to evolve into a being with no thirst, no hunger, no desires, no imaginations, no ecstasies and no regrets. I did not want to die anymore, because death did not hold any meaning, a life in which I could collect all the goodness of the world, convert it into a recipe filled with strength, joy and happiness and extend it to those who needed to witness the miracles of love and unselfishness had to be led. It was an awakening that I had never contemplated.

41

He had been a businessman, I thought, a nomadic businessman, someone I had heard of in my childhood stories, for there was no village or a town he did not know of, he also seemed to be a genius with exemplary talking skills. Awfully determined on hiring me, he offered to shelter me in his outhouse that night to give me a little more time to decide if I wanted to work with him. However, I walked back to my small home with a promise to see him the next morning. He could have never figured out my motive to go back, my latest acquaintance had been waiting for me next door.

Nafisa Bee. She was rare enough a person to have not got surprised when I asked her for some bread after failing to find anything to eat nearby.

"You do not intend to stay here longer?" was her first question to me.

"Not sure, but may be for a few months, I need to earn some money for my onward journey, and I have none on me right now," I had replied.

"Exactly, it looks like you have been on a journey for very long."

I was not too surprised, she looked like one who had been on a much longer journey than mine, and journeys happen in each one's life, some with long distances and some with longer moments, I thought.

"Yes, it has been—years now, I travelled with an intention, not clear what it really was at the beginning, a lot has got decrypted gradually," I responded.

"Only premature minds have the ability to gauge, but many of us start realizing the causes and purpose of moving from one destination to the other as we mature," she said with a smile.

Walking down the street the morning after I had figured out the shop the old lady had spoken of. I went and stood there for some time till I gathered the attention of the owner.

"I am in search of some work, so was wondering if I could do something for you," I said.

"Not really, I do not have anything for you right now, you could come after some days and check again if I need any assistance in anything," he said.

I was quite prepared for the reply; because the old lady had assured me that he may not consider me immediately and would find out my whereabouts first. I thought of asking her for teaching somewhere, as I had done in Yazd, but ironically, in this town I would fit more for being a pupil rather than teaching others. The only thing I was suited best for was teaching Arabic and the Holy Quran; however, I was hesitant to speak my mind so easily. Having interacted with her for three days, I thought I knew her too well to hesitate and think so much.

After walking back from the market place, I went back and knocked her door in anticipation of a wonderful warm smile. But there was no reply after knocking for a few minutes; I realized that the door lay slightly open. I pushed the door and peeped inside, it was dark and she had not lit the evening lamp as I had seen her doing the previous evening. I gathered the courage, I walked inside and found that she lay in her bed, ailing and waiting for someone to give her water.

"My angel child, you have been sent to hear me in my last moments," she said.

"Don't worry, now that I am here, I will look after you and make you hale and hearty again, nothing will happen to you," I responded, despite the intuition that she was talking the truth. I wondered if I was cheating her by saying that, but I chose to encourage her rather than accepting what she said.

"Your wishes and prayers are genuine, but I know that my end is nearing and I am happy that I am able to speak to you," she said.

I sat by her bedside.

"You have seen enough of the world now, it is time for you to go and take charge of your duties you have travelled for from so far," she said.

"What duties?" I questioned her with a surprise.

"You were to meet the strugglers to see how they dealt with their day to day life, you have lived with the traders and understood what trade was intended for, you also met aspirers who had the vision of becoming reformers and wanted to turn the world into a better place, you got yourself completely influenced by the recluse, the crusaders made you feel guilty that you were not doing enough for the world, and the givers led you to increased generosity," she said.

Benazir Patil

She was uttering such familiar concepts, I had heard this before, a story of my childhood, a story of seven kinds of people I were to meet, but she had only talked of six.

"What has all this to do with the duties that I am supposed to be doing?" I asked her again.

"A lot!" she exclaimed, took a pause, smiled at me, and continued.

"Because you have yet to meet the healer, only after meeting the healer, will you realize and identify with yourself, will understand that you are a healer too, the six kinds of people you met with, appeared so different, you could identify with none of them."

"Strange, and where am I going to meet this healer, do you know of any?" I laughed at my serious question.

"If you have met the other six, you surely will be meeting the seventh kind too," she said.

I had known nothing about her life, was she herself that healer she was referring to? Confusion and curiosity walked into my mind at once.

"What makes you think that I have the strength to heal the people of their wounds, I have myself just come out of a wound and it was indeed a difficult process," I asked her.

"Suffering is an endless phenomenon, but suffering is also a perception, the people who taught the world how to end their sufferings did not destroy the sufferings really, they just helped people cope with their losses, healed them to generate more strength, and reinstated a vigour to perceive life differently," she said.

Everything she said seemed so obvious to me, yet I had questions for her.

"And what am I supposed to do now?" I asked her.

"You are supposed to just continue with your journey, until you meet the seventh kind, as you realize your strength, your will have found your path," she said.

Memories collided inside me one after the other—suffering indeed existed in many forms. I sat in silence for a few minutes, thinking about the suffering I had witnessed in Gujranwala, all the suffering had just got filled into my empty mind, and I had worked hard on healing myself of those, I wondered if I was capable of healing others of that.

Perhaps Nafisa Bee could tell me how I was to do that.

"So you know yourself how to heal the people of their suffering?" I asked her.

She turned to me and pulled me a little closer with her weak hands, she placed her trembling hands on my head and looked into my eyes, before I could even ask her what she wanted she breathed her last.

Two days later, I went to the shop as promised, I happened to meet both the owners, realized later that they were father and son, before that I had met both of them separately on different occasions but in the same shop. It was a well-managed printing press. The elder owner introduced me to his son and asked me if I was willing to start work immediately. I unhesitatingly accepted the deal, though at the back of my beyond I was not sure how long I was going to work with them; nevertheless, I had to have some work.

Benazir Patil

I had never worked with any printer earlier, but he had given me serious lessons on how to work efficiently regardless of where one worked.

In the next few days I had picked up enough speed and was being paid wages on a weekly basis. I had left the room I was housed in and had started staying in the room where Nafisa bee was staying. I had also made friends with some people around and had started exchanging thoughts in my broken language.

"Was not the war that occurred years ago a war of total destruction," Mehboob asked us.

I had become a part of a small group that sat together in the evenings with a dim lantern around.

"The war was over but perhaps peace has never returned since," said Sukhram.

"How safe and established everything was till a few years ago. We used to talk then that some big war is coming but none of us had imagined it to be like that," said Lala Harshal.

"Life was comfortable and safe once upon a time, but things are changing now," he said.

Some of them were real men of knowledge, they comprehended the world with a different eye, but some like Sukhram were men of spiritual inclination. With just a few questions, their perspective was visible and they were honest enough to accept that talking about war all the time would not help anymore; they had to do something to bring back the language of peace.

"I feel tired of thinking and talking about wars, I feel as if half of my life has just gone in witnessing the terror. I feel it has been thirty years now that we all have lived with this misery called wars," he said.

Ironically, in different parts of the world men had continuously come together to measure the worth of all the bloodshed in terms of the gains their natives were making out of this loss. Patriotism was fetching the best profits ever and this was a new business that men wanted to venture into.

It was in the wake of one such war I had lived in Shivani's house, the memories of my conversation with Satviki flooded my mind.

42

My pursuit for divinity had vanished; I could incessantly perceive the almighty in the people I met, the places I reached, and the trials I got intertwined with.

"Just the way we struggle to find His presence, God also looks forward to determine His presence in our lives. Trying to search for Him in specific places is futile, despite knowing the truth that God only cares for his knowledge of Him and nothing else, man has deliberately created innumerable places of worship," Shivani had once shared with me.

Erasing her physical image from my mind, I could never attempt, the attachment with her soul was nonetheless instinctive. The thought of having lost her forever and her myriad reminiscences drew me closer to her. The language of distance had become extinct; affection was mounting as high and as rapidly that knew no boundaries. Never had I experienced such a complete sense of oneness with any other earthly soul. My conviction of spiritual actuality had got reinforced.

How strange it was to have found peace in a feeling I had never experienced before? For the first time in my life I was scribbling something, thoughts that were not mine, but hers, beliefs that were gifted to me while I stayed as a stranger in their house. My only precious possessions, my heart inspired me to speak them out to the world. That was to become my contribution to the *Ketaab-e-Hayaat* I imagined.

"All of us are born with a freedom to act as we feel and desire, but that is not all, we have a soul inside this physical frame that guides us to the truth, and no soul has reached the stage of perfection, it evolves based on our experiences, the experience of suffering and happiness lets us evolve incessantly," I penned one of her thoughts on paper.

As time passed, an impression had started embedding inside me.

I had mastered the art of going beyond hopes, fears and excitements, my soul truly sought mindfulness amidst all the uncertainties. The solitude of my mind was no more a menace; it was indeed a trial filled with faith.

With a complete sense of calmness, I opened the *Ketaab-e-Hayaat,* Page 223, it read:

> *The labyrinth is a pathway to God with a simple seven-circuit archetypal pattern, a clearly defined center and one entrance. It leads you back to the beginning despite all the twists and turns.*
>
> *Walking among the turnings, one loses track of direction and of the outside world, and thus quiets the mind. It helps you find a correct path through life, bypassing many misleading sideways.*
>
> *A journey through the labyrinth has three phases:*
> *"Surrender"—the beginning of your journey is a time to release, let go of the daily struggles, worries, thoughts and fears. This act of shedding what blocks you or holds you back allows the mind to quiet, open and begin emptying.*
> *"Illumination"—being open upon reaching the center of the labyrinth you touch your center and receive the guidance and light that Spirit has for you.*

"Integration"—As you follow the path away from the center of the labyrinth the light/guidance received begins to integrate into your life and service.

The structure of the ancient seven-path labyrinth contains a semi-circular center, surrounded by seven paths contained within the boundaries of a larger circle. This is based on the belief that Earth is the center of the Universe with the seven planets orbiting around it.

It is a journey that leaves day-to-day life behind. It is a journey that sets aside all ambitions and concerns. It is a journey to that place where God's people worship in spirit and in truth; a journey to a deeper faith.

I pondered over my journey; I was heading to the next destination, without much awareness that it was to be the seventh one.

Then Peter came to Jesus and asked, "Lord, how many times shall I forgive my brother when he sins against me? Up to seven times?"

Jesus answered, "I tell you, not seven times, but seventy times seven".

43

The seventh destination had finally arrived. My destiny had kindly made its way to the other six; those were equally unplanned as the seventh. To be well thought, well said, and well done was something I had planned when I initiated this flight.

Throughout my life I had harbored the idea of becoming a better human being, without ever having an ideal that I wanted to be like. Bestowed by sufficient intellect to pave our paths, I believed none of us needed one. Admiration for those who left their mark on my mind was nevertheless a mutual human attribute I esteemed in myself.

The transformation in me was another aspect I constantly peeped into. The meticulous sense of the almighty amazed me. My mind continued to step into two boats at the same time; while walking towards the shrine too I pondered about the two carefree men who had brought me from the station, and also got merged with the strange reflections of all those I had met with in the past.

All in the universe is a part of the design, putting the fish out of water and the birds out of skies could have never worked, it would be a departure severe enough to cause immense misery to them. With a defined abode for each of us, we all remain blessed with some fabulous qualities, no different from the animals. Despite all the wisdom that flowed from one corner of the world to another, all prophets struggled to reveal just one thing: the original nature of man, how it got lost, and what were the ways to recover it. Preaching a route of spiritual discipline was not something unusual, it was akin to living a life with nature just as the fish and birds did.

As I continued to walk conversing with myself, I suddenly felt like a tiny creature; the colossal doorway I faced had compelled this feeling of a shrunken self. Overwhelmed, I entered and found myself approaching the shrine.

Built by a king, history had diverse tales to tell about the city. Fatehpur literally meant the city of victory. Some believed that the Sufi dwelled here a few centuries ago. Gradually the news of his healing powers spread, attracted by his sagacity and mystical consciousness people started settling around the shrine. Some also believed that the Sufi's blessing to the king had encouraged him to populate the city.

I walked up to the tomb that stood in the centre of an open land fenced by fortified walls. Suddenly, I felt encircled into the foray of vibrations Zeba had talked about.

"So you have come to tie the thread?" Someone questioned.

I had no clue what he was talking about, but the curiosity to know more inspired my interaction

"Thread?" I asked him.

"Many people do that, it's a tradition here, see that screen," he pointed at the neatly carved marble walls which had uncountable knotted threads tied on it.

"Tie the thread and share your wish with Baba, it will surely come true," he added with an understanding of my unawareness.

Benazir Patil

I was not surprised; conventions like this were not unknown to me.

"And what was Baba's own belief?" I asked him.

"His message stood in solitude: 'serving humanity is the highest form of commitment to the almighty,'" he responded.

"This is so true, are you his disciple?" I asked him with a smile.

"Yes, I have been living here for last eighteen years."

"That is a pretty long time."

"I lived miles away, but somehow reached here. Are you a tourist?" he asked me.

"No, perhaps I have also reached here, like you have, for some reason."

"Here, take this, would you like to tie the thread there?" Someone patted my back and asked thinking that I was waiting there pondering about my wish I had come to fulfil. Back home too I had seen people tying *dakils* to reverent trees called *darakht-e-morad* located in sacred sights, connected to holy personages.

"Sure, why not, let me."

I thought about my wish, I had none, as I went about tying it I realized I had been robbed of all my thoughts except for that of Shivani's.

"Do you know someone in town?"

"Yes .... you ...," I replied with a smile.

"My name is Raghuram and yours?" he asked instantly.

"Khudabakhsh."

Bonded by an instant liking for each other, we spoke about several things in and around Fatehpur. He offered me to stay in his place till I found a place for myself; I gladly accepted it and went along. Sitting in his house, I stretched my eyes to the horizon. After a hot cup of tea, I felt awakened. For long, I had just been journeying, often tempted, I had refrained from opening the radiant clothed book I carried, I finally opened it and reached Page 70, it read:

Those seven weeks of Buddha

In the first week after enlightenment, he sat under the bodhi tree experiencing the happiness of freedom and peace.

In the second week, in thanks and gratitude to the tree that had sheltered him during his struggle for Buddhahood, he stood without moving his eyes as he meditated on the bodhi tree.

In the third week, he saw through his mind's eye that the gods in the heavens were not sure whether he had attained enlightenment or not. To prove his enlightenment he created a golden bridge in the air and walked up and down on it for a whole week.

In the fourth week, he created a beautiful jewelled chamber and sitting inside it meditated on 'Abhidhamma' the "Detailed Teaching". His mind and body were so purified that six coloured rays came out of his body — blue, yellow, red, white, orange and a mixture of these five. Each colour

Benazir Patil

represented each of his noble qualities: yellow for holiness, white for purity, blue for confidence, red for wisdom and orange for desirelessness. The mixed colour represented all these noble qualities.

In the fifth week, while meditating under a banyan tree, three most charming girls called Tanha, Rati and Raga came to disturb his meditation through their dance and charm, he continued to meditate unperturbed, and soon they got tired and left him alone.

In the sixth week he went and meditated at the foot of a mucalinda tree. It began to rain heavily and a huge king cobra came out and coiled his body seven times to keep him warm and placed his hood over his head to protect him from the rain. After seven days the rain stopped and the snake changed into a young man who paid his respects to the Buddha. The Buddha then said:

"Happy are they who are contented. Happiness is for those who hear and know the truth. Happy are they who have good will in this world towards all sentient beings. Happy are they who have no attachments and have passed beyond sense-desires. The disappearance of the word "I AM" is indeed the highest happiness."

In the seventh week, he meditated under the rajayatana tree. On the fiftieth morning, after seven weeks of fasting, two merchants came into his presence. They were called Tapussa and Bhallika. They offered him rice cakes and honey to break his fast and the Buddha told them some of what he had found in his enlightenment. These two merchants, by taking refuge in the Buddha and his Dharma became the first lay followers.

I read it three times, closed the book, looked at Raghuram and thought of his kindness.

That was my first evening with Raghuram; he narrated me myriad stories of his life and made me feel as if our meeting on that day was nothing but a reunion. At times simply hearing an account of something that has transpired in another person's life can set off our intellect thinking and we actually mirror how we would feel if we were to be a part of that experience ourselves. Interestingly, we assume that we are on an infinite expedition, neither wishing nor intending to anticipate that this will ever end; liveliness in us gets equated with our struggle to stay happy in a world that gets more and more challenging for us. What antiquity passed on to us does not hold true completely, that the wise learn from other people's mistakes and fools from their own; there are many who prefer to remain fools and go through the experience to turn wiser than the wise who learned from others.

"I need to find some work for my living," I told Raghuram the following morning.

"What work? Now that you are here, you should be serving people and that's it, that is what I do," he responded in surprise.

"I agree, but I also need to do some work to pay for my living expenses, isn't that required?"

"What work can you do?"

"I can do anything; work as helper, teacher or even keeping accounts of a businessman."

"Let me talk to some people I know, meanwhile, let me introduce you to some friends who work with me at the shrine," he said.

I followed him blindly, until we reached the shrine. I spotted a man with a water jug on his hand; he was busy asking people if they wanted water, without even uttering a word.

"Who is this man?"

"He is Kareem, he does this the whole day, and you will always find him offering water to people."

"Is he not able to talk?"

"Nobody has heard him talking, but he is not dumb, he can talk, he has been here for years together, even before I came here."

"What could be the reason for his quietness?" I murmured to myself.

"That's a long story, not many people know about it"

"What is that?"

"Kareem's parents loved him and always did what they thought was best, but an incident changed everything for him, and for last twenty years he has been living a life of a recluse in the vicinity of the shrine. He had a brother, younger to him by eight years, life was complete fun when they were together, both, fond of swimming, often went to the nearby lake and swam for hours. One day, as they began to swim, the younger one got flown into a deeper belt of the lake, lost complete control and despite several attempts of Kareem, got drowned. Kareem was barely seventeen, deep inside he cursed himself for his failure to save his brother, but much worse happened when his parents cursed him too."

"Then?"

"With a sunken nervousness, he held himself responsible for his brother's tragic death. A complete loss of self esteem and self confidence attacked him through and through his every vein. He left home one day in search of solace. Life had come to a halt for him: after the loss, he could not excel in his studies either and finally landed as a worker with a merchant who kept him with a word of sympathy. But nobody knows how he reached here," Raghuram concluded.

"Matters of life and death too are dominated by the supremacy of the tongue," I said.

"How?"

"The words uttered have the power to create and to destroy. In the scriptures we are warned that the words that affect someone's life and cause someone's death will be accounted for in the book of our life." I added.

"But words can also be virtuous," said Raghuram.

"Yes, words have the power to heal and nurture goodness too; it's important to use words carefully."

I could comprehend the guilt Kareem had been living with for years together; my mind imagined his world.

Unfolding my own thoughts had led to a longer pause, but before Raghuram could say anything, I continued sharing my thoughts.

"Usually people hold onto their bad experiences. This not only compels them to go through the misery of that experience, but also keeps them locked in the past preventing them from entering their present. Since our life experiences shape the type of person we become, we are unable to

Benazir Patil

change the way we feel until we are able to resolve those past unanswered questions by creating new life experiences for ourselves. The reason for this is that every experience we have in life creates a belief in our minds and these beliefs cause us to behave and react in one way or another further influencing our future thoughts. If we have a bad experience, a belief related to that experience gets created, and it continues to influence us throughout our entire life."

Raghuram patiently looked at me.

"We all have been created from the same essence, when one of us is in pain, the others cannot rest, and if we do not care about the pain others go through, we insult the very humanity, Zeba always told me." I said

"Who Zeba?"

"My mother," I smiled and said. He was perhaps perturbed about the fact that I called my mother by her name—many people had reacted like this in the past.

Talking about Zeba, by and by, had become my habit over the years. Be it by the fire, at the setting sun, in the midst of the crowd or in the market places of the villages I walked, every event of my life reminded me something that she had told me, taught me or even warned me about.

"Don't you think, sometimes just the impressions on your mind are so influential that you cannot distinguish them from actual remembrance and sometimes just the observations are so powerful that they get transformed into experiences?," he asked.

"For me it has been more to do with observations and assimilating them into my mind," I responded.

"And what were those?"

"Probably observing every person that I have met in life, understand their motives behind the life they led, and grasping the course of events and consequences of their journeys"

"And what did you gather from it?"

"Very few listen to their inner voices, some react to the happenings around them, some find it difficult to understand what their lives are meant for and some are completely inebriated in achieving the worldly gains and falsely consider themselves as the kings who rule the world."

"How did this matter to you, was it an important learning?"

"We have lived through a history of thousands of years, and we still cannot say that we have learned it all; we are still learning, had experiences influenced us so much, we would have continued improving with the influx of new descendants, but history reflects just the contrary, degeneration seems inevitable with the onset of every new generation," I responded.

"So your experience tells you that men do not learn from their experiences, is it?" Raghuram asked with a mischievous smile, with a motive to drag me into a dense discussion.

"Yes, may be, if only one is conscious and wakeful, one can fruitfully move through an experience. Without an alert mind, it is futile to understand what one is going through and where one is leading to," I concluded.

Benazir Patil

44

Commonly understood as a vagabond, most of them assumed that I had come to the shrine for a specific reason, and I would soon be going back to my place. Little did they know that there was neither a place owned by me nor had I discovered one I did not belong to.

I had lived near rivers and mountains, farmlands and deserts. Sometimes in the midst of complete silence and sometimes surrounded by the crowd, I had evolved into a likely creature with a culture of my own; my culture unfolded the account of not just humanity, but it also unearthed the existence of the almighty. Nonetheless, I belonged to the same human race that professed interest in digging up everything that was buried off ages ago; I was simply one of the generations of the same civilization who did not feel exhausted by exploring all that I could.

Raghuram helped me find a small place to stay. Different people visited the shrine every day. The thought of talking to Kareem lay constantly at the back of my mind. He quietly observed me prostrating to Mother Earth, so did Raghuram, but unlike Kareem, his inquisitiveness compelled him to question me.

"Are these some different prayers?" he asked.

"I am listening to what Mother Earth is saying," I smiled and replied.

"I didn't get you."

"We have been created from the earth. If we are aware of our origin, we will not have any place for arrogance and pride in our lives, because we know that we come from this same mud."

"But, what were you trying to hear?"

"Mother Earth was talking about different laws of life."

"Laws of life? Like?"

"Like the Law of One."

"Law of One?"

"It is simple: all is One, all has been created by 'One', we all belong to that One sole creator."

"Indeed, it is strange, despite being so different from each other, we all are supposed to be the same, belonging to one creator."

"Raghu, I will explain to you some day about how we evolve till the seventh density and how our minds and bodies merge back into our creator."

I noticed that Kareem was ardently attentive to our talks. He often did that. Everytime I saw him, I tried my best to reach out to him with efforts to negate his feelings of nothingness.

"Kareem, if we realize our abilities, we can build a better world. If we cannot accept ourselves with our limitations, how can we ever accept others around us? If we are unable to accept and trust them, how will we respect and love them? And when we do not extend that love to others, how will it ever come back to us?"

Benazir Patil

Shockingly, he looked at me.

"You tried your best to save your brother, but the almighty had different plans, on which you had no control, there are many situations in our lives of which we cannot do anything about, and have to accept the pre-written verdicts."

I asked Kareem to prostrate and listen to Mother Earth, when he got up, I could observe his mesmerized look and said, "We need to know that earth is our mother, do you recall how much we speak to and cling to our mother as a child, our Mother Earth also longs for our clinging to her and talking to her, she waits for us, it is we who forget her."

"Is this the way you cling to her," Kareem's eyes reflected radiance.

"Yes, indeed, this is the way I become one with her."

Suddenly, my eyes flashed the same image I had often dreamt. The image of Daniyaal reading a huge book; so huge that it was held on the back of another person, while Daniyaal sat and read it intensely. I disconnected myself from that frequent revelation thinking that it was he who had informed me about the right time assigned for every understanding that came my way. Perhaps it had some connection with the *Ketab-e-Hayaat* I possessed.

Intermittently, I met visitors, who approached me to spell out things that led me to accompany them to the voice of Mother Earth. Inquisitive souls enquired about the sorcerer who could listen to Mother Earth and felt astonished after meeting with a slender and quiet person like me.

On and off I found someone standing in front of me, waiting to know what listening to Mother Earth meant.

"It is all about your relationship with this loam," I would explain.

"You are a part of this earth on which you stand, you breathe this air without which your existence is bleak, you flaunt in this sunlight without which you cannot identify and understand anything and you still think that the universe is mysterious, you never want to understand the universe and its ways, because you think you are apart from it, rather than a part of it. There is nothing novel about it, we all have had lessons about our connection with god, Mother Earth is no different."

One morning while I was interacting with a young man a child standing by him found my explanation about this connection vague and weird, hesitatingly, he asked me,

"Khuda, I always wonder, there are so many people living on this earth, but all are different, nobody similar to the other. Can we ask Mother Earth about it?"

His thought did not estrange me; as a child, I often had these questions, I recalled the story I had read in the *Ketaab-e-Hayaat.*

"Long years ago, there existed just one united humanity, resembling each other and speaking a single language, they migrated from the east and reached the land of Shinar"

"Where is that?" he interrupted.

"Somewhere near Babylon"

"One day they decided to build a city with a tower whose top may reach unto heaven, so that it helps them reach the god almighty by walking up above."

"Oh, how interesting, can I go to the tower, even I would like to reach to God."

I smiled and continued, "God heard their talks and wondered that with their sense and strength of unity, they were capable of doing that, so he just picked all of them and scattered them upon the face of the Earth, and confused their languages, and they left off building the city, which was called Babel."

"But why did God do that?" the child asked seemingly agitated.

"Humankind was entering the arena of arrogance, they thought that they could reach heaven by building a stair-case to it," I responded with a smile.

"But wasn't that a great idea?"

"No, the moment a man feels he is self-sufficient, he loses the sight of the almighty and thinks he is capable of doing anything without his grace."

He stood there with more questions in his mind.

"Remember this story and the truth that all your capabilities are but a gift of the almighty."

Many felt I was foolish, but many, when heard her truly, felt delighted, felt tempted to know more about it and they listened to me with keenness. My words fell upon their ears as some melody. People came from far and wide; they thought I had some divine connection. I explained to them that there was nothing new and that they could do this all by themselves, but strangely, a glory had started spreading, perhaps Mother Earth herself was instrumental in doing that, people wanted to learn it from me alone.

I also poured all my sentiments, my eyes naturally reflected the reverence, I compensated for the admiration their minds nurtured.

And I often overheard, "There, inside the shrine, resides Khuda, who taught us to listen to Mother Earth"

Benazir Patil

45

Time journeyed by itself. I hardly paid any heed to the passing days. One day, someone told me the story of a blessed soul in the town, meeting whom was like having been for a pilgrimage. People who conceptualized holiness only in terms of edifices and orders, felt ashamed of their thoughts when they met with her. She had come a long way spreading the divine message; it was not the givens of the place that mattered, her sanguinity and her commitment to humanity made all the difference.

"Raghuram, it has been years, I have often heard of this person but it never occurred to me to find out who this silent saint is? Have you ever met her?"

"You mean Abdul Rahim's daughter?" asked Raghuram.

"The silent saint! That's what I have heard of."

"Indeed, I am also talking about the same person. Here, read this," he put his left hand in the side pocket of his cloak and opened out a small chit that lay rolled up in his hand purse. He extended that piece of paper to me.

"We are born blank; we are then dressed by different attitudes, opinions and ideas, some make us feel strong and some add vulnerability to our being. Just shed off the robe of worry and weakness, and wear the attitude of intimacy with god"

"What a mighty thought!" I exclaimed

"Yes, once I was very disturbed and just walked to the *ashram* to meet her. Ayesha just looked at me, scribbled this on a piece of paper and gave it to me".

Suddenly, a contradiction ran inside me: I was always confused with the question whether each of us is born with a defined purpose and then we work towards finding the meaning of this purpose through some introspection or there was something more to it?

"What happened?"

Raghuram's question perplexed me.

"Raghuram, I have heard of only two kinds of mystics: one, who were sent by God to reveal some decrees to the world; and the other, who did not enunciate new laws but engaged the world to follow the divine decrees. I was wondering which creed Ayesha belonged to," I told him.

Raghuram hardly understood what I asked. He continued with his explanation.

"I may have visited Abdul Rahim's house several times, a rich businessman he was, but it is only in the last few years that I have seen his daughter Ayesha helping all those who went to her. In fact, I have often thought if his death had caused her to become like this," he ignored my question and continued.

"Like what?"

"Like . . . . someone from the other world!"

"Other world?"

"Yes, she is not like us, she is different!"

"And who looks after the *ashram*?"

"Abdul Rahim's elder brother, Abdul Razzaq, he takes care of Ayesha as well; both her parents are no more, they passed away a few years ago."

"How often have you met her?"

"Actually, many times. I have often visited the *ashram* to meet with Abdul Razzaq for some or the other work. In-fact, one other time also she had shared her wonderful thoughts with me." Let me show you something," he got up to open a wooden box kept in the corner of his room.

"See, read this. This is the time when there were some skirmishes in the town and I had stayed at the *ashram* for a night as I felt somewhat insecure about those tensions."

"What tensions?"

"There were some tensions between the two factions in the town. That day I said to her, I wish there were no religions in this world, and this is what she wrote for me." Raghuram handed over the piece of paper that was neatly kept in the diary, which was safely preserved in the box.

It was written: "Though the world has defined many religions, it is actually our deeds that define the religion we belong to; if we do the deed of giving, we belong to the religion of givers, and our message is that of giving and revealing the law of giving to this universe. And what it does to our lives is the obligation we accept."

It was a deep thought, something which Zeba and Nafisa Bee had explained to me. I felt rather curious and keen to sense the aura of such a blessed soul. However, I marvelled if her silence conveyed her thoughts more strongly than her words did. I tried my best to learn the reasons behind her silence, but finally consoled myself that I would have to go and meet her to understand what it meant.

46

I entered the *ashram*.

The vibrations were inconceivable; something that Mother Earth was transmitting without me questioning her about anything. A vision appeared, as though my own spirit was watching me from a distance, reminding me of my moments of spiritual thirst. A want of seeking serenity to fulfil the enigmatic questions tangled with moments of bitterness, sweetness and indifference. Sweetness definitely emanated a feeling of happiness but bitterness pushed me into a profound sense of gratitude and exposed me to the impermanence of pleasure and pain.

An unusual appearance of all the sentiments at once was difficult to handle.

I had already walked a few steps; I found myself standing in a sufficiently large room—it appeared to be a dormitory. After having waited for some time, Yashwant, the in-charge, asked me if I wanted to write down my details in a long book; he had assumed that I had come there for shelter.

He questioned me about my whereabouts.

"Khudabakhsh," I said.

"Khudabakhsh, is it, it sounds like you are . . . ?" he questioned me.

"Yes, you are right! But now, I practise the religion of loving and giving," I exclaimed and smiled.

He looked at me as if I had uttered something untoward.

"And you come from?" he further asked.

"I am a traveller, I come from nowhere and will be going nowhere, the world lies inside me as much as it lies outside of me, I feel I belong to nature, and nature is infinite, without any boundaries, so I belong to this infinity," I told him.

As soon as I saw his bewildered expression I realized my folly but kept quiet

By then, Ramdin, one of the other attendants of the *ashram* had also walked in. Yashwant assured me that if I required any help, Ramdin would be able to help, and left immediately.

"Though it looks like you have travelled from far, you do not seem to have any luggage with you?" asked Ramdin.

"All of us are a part of a procession on this earth since the time we are born. Everything is created by the almighty and remains His; we mistake ourselves all the time by calling it our own, each of us is aware of the fact that we are born empty handed and go back to this earth without taking anything with us," I shared with him along with a smile.

He looked as taken aback as Yashwant. He further enquired with me if I had been to the *ashram* ever before, exchanged a few more words, and asked me to wait in a prayer hall.

Before starting for the *ashram*, my mind was restless; I had then taken to the *Ketaab-e-Hayaat* to understand this confused state of mind.

I referred to Page 106, it read:

Benazir Patil

The 'cubit' is nothing but 28 digits with lines at every fourth digit representing the 'palm', it is the seven palms that make one cubit, and the cubit is the most accurate measurement.

"Which of you by taking thought can add one cubit unto his stature?"

We each receive a portion of eternity within which we must make our mark.

We have a given time span, and anxiety cannot increase its length.

We are anxious about our future, our old age, and all the comforts of tomorrow.

None of us can add more age, more comfort and more treasures to our allotted life.

I sat in the hall with complete quietness. After some time, I prostrated to Mother Earth and heard her peacefully, she reminded me of the weird vibrations when I had entered the campus. She intimated me to be more attentive to my surroundings, but I let myself be, I needed to calm myself, I had sensed my heartbeats, something had overwhelmed me enormously.

Just then I realized someone talking to me, "She often scribbles the first seven verses of the Quran."

"In Arabic?" I asked.

"No, not in Arabic, in Hindustani script," he said.

"Hindustani?" I was a little startled and did not hesitate in displaying my surprise to the stranger. He had noticed me waiting in the hall and had come forward to make me comfortable in that alien place, letting me know about Ayesha and her knowledge of the Holy Quran was his way of making me feel at home. He left the hall with a smile without responding; he assumed it was an expression and not a question at all.

I felt a little lost, wondering why I had come to this place.

Ayesha entered the hall and sat in front of me, watching me patiently. I felt as if someone was pumping some kind of energy into my soul, an unexpected blessedness had overpowered me; I lifted my head more slightly to observe her face.

She also raised her absorbing eyes and looked at me.

The astonishment was profound. The winds, the sun, Mother Earth, all were observing my chaotic soul. My mind flew through the abyss to a place where I had lived years ago; the thoughts were faster than lightning, attracting my attention to her charisma, her appearance, I was struggling, fighting the impossible, for now this could not have been the 'Ayesha' I was to meet.

Was this fiction or a pretense? Mother Earth couldn't be intimating me of this.

Her compassion helped in waning my bizarre expression, in a few moments, our eyes started conversing with each other. She continued to gaze at me, it was apparent; several thoughts were rustling inside her being too.

Both of us sat there unperturbed, while many passed us by without paying any attention. I could sense her eagerness to respond to the ethereal joy she had witnessed in my eyes.

Benazir Patil

My speechlessness had assured her that I was the same silent creature who had lived an unknown life once upon a time.

Her silence seemed unreal. It had taken her no time to confirm who I was. I could not identify the slightest of change in her face or her expression, there seemed to be a minutely added maturity that had made her more graceful than before.

Suddenly, I heard her saying, "I know you."

But the very next moment I realized it was just an illusion, she continued to sit in profound silence.

After much resistance I opened up and uttered, "Ayesha, I need no evidence, neither a witness to make me believe that you are the same blessed soul!"

My speech shocked her immensely, but she continued to listen.

"There are many laws of this universe, but the most effective is the law of causation, every change in the universe has its cause and both the causes and its effects are nothing but unbroken chains. Losing you had its own basis and finding you back would definitely be having its own reasons."

Ironically, our parting in the past was like a conspiracy designed by the almighty. However, the conspiracy of the day had left her with no understanding of the past.

I told her all about myself without waiting for a response. I assumed the silence was momentary. I took her leave with a commitment to come again the next day.

Fourteen years had passed.

As I walked back to the gate, I saw a man approaching me; he came close and asked me, "You seem to be new here."

"I am staying here for the last 7 years."

"Here, meaning?"

"In Fatehpur."

"Ok."

"What brought you here?"

"I generally serve the people who come to the shrine."

"That's wonderful, god bless you."

"Both of us exchanged smiles and parted.

Something lay hidden behind the quiet eyes. Suddenly, I realized that I was a changed person, long years ago, I had been an intensely inquisitive soul, but the *Ketaab-e-Hayaat* had taught me that god had his own ways of revealing the truth and destiny ruled the timing of that.

The ecstasy of seeing her was unbearable, for the first time I felt that even the moments of joy had the nerve to make me feel miserable. I bent down and prostrated to Mother Earth; nobody else had the capability to fathom my intense emotions.

"You have the power to heal her, heal her from all that she has been through," resonated Mother Earth.

I was a little startled. Healing her from what? My mind questioned. I did not ponder much and waited for the understanding to come.

I got up and walked back to my dwelling.

"You had been to the *ashram*, I heard?" Raghuram questioned me.

"Yes."

"Were you able to meet the saintly soul?"

"Yes" I said again.

"They say that she is the author of divine prayers."

"Yes, indeed she is," I responded.

Nafisa bee's intimation about my meeting with a healer echoed again. But it simply conflicted with what Mother Earth had just instructed.

47

The initial perplexity had turned into immense joy. But the joy, seemed, decidedly one-sided. I felt as if I was running to her with a sobbing cry of happiness and had gathered her close.

The thoughts fluctuated from one extreme to the other. After much twisting and turning, I sat up in the bed and opened the *Ketaab-e-Hayaat*, I reached Page 205, and it read:

> *And when he had opened the seventh seal, there was silence in heaven about the space of half an hour.*
>
> *And I saw the seven angels, which stood before God; and to them were given seven trumpets.*
>
> *And the seven angels who had the seven trumpets prepared themselves to sound.*
>
> *And I heard a great voice out of the temple saying to the seven angels, Go your ways, and pour out the vials of the wrath of God upon the earth.*

I did not understand anything, neither did I re-read, my mind did not allow me to do that.

As promised, I reached the *ashram* the next morning. There seemed to be nobody to take my cognizance. I too walked in seamlessly without any hesitation. Suddenly, I spotted the old man who had greeted me yesterday, he seemed to be interested in talking to me.

"I am Abdul Razzaq, this place belongs to my younger brother, and Ayesha is my niece". He said.

"I am Khudabakhsh" I acknowledged with a smile and said.

"I wanted to ask you yesterday about the man in the shrine who makes you hear the Mother Earth, have you met him, it has been long that I had been wanting to meet him."

I was taken aback with his question, of which I had no anticipation whatsoever. In the shrine too, people often walked up to me in search of such a man. Likewise, today too my modesty instilled a strange consciousness in me.

"Yes, that person is me, I am the one who tries to teach this, when people are keen and willing" I responded with deep humility

"Oh! What a wonderful thing to happen" he said with absolute enthusiasm.

"Every time I heard about you, I told Ayesha that one day we will invite you here and she always had a welcoming smile". He said

Abdul Razzaq confirmed what people generally shared that Ayesha was an epitome of silence.

"Khudabakhsh, you must teach us to listen to the Mother Earth"

"Yes I will" I responded with a smile and both of us parted again

He didn't seem to be inquisitive about my consecutive visit to their place on the very next day. In fact he cut short the conversation so that I move on to discuss more with Ayesha.

As I entered the prayer hall, I saw Ayesha meditating; her closed eyes expressed more than the open ones could speak.

As I looked at her, I felt as if she had been waiting eagerly to see me since our parting yesterday. I sat there quietly, waiting for her to become conscious again.

Ayesha opened her eyes, it was a deep look; she almost questioned me about my arrival.

I began sharing with her about the bond I had developed with her parents after she had left for Lahore.

"Ironically, the day you left for Lahore, the very next morning, I had regained my memory and was able to talk my heart out to your parents, I stayed with them for few more months, assisting them and looking after home, but some day, I had to resume my journey for I always wanted to come to Fatehpur" I said

"You must be wondering, why Fatehpur of all the places?. I was fourteen when my mother passed away, she was born in Fathepur and always wanted me to come here, for reasons I am yet to discover" I added

I spoke endlessly about Satviki and the prayer-man, the delight in her eyes was layered with enigmatic misery.

"You indeed took time to recognize me, in those few months you must have met me often, but as a healer, you focused more on my chakras. Lack of conversation between us would have erased my image from my mind" I said

"For me, though, every word of yours impacted my mind, the thoughts expressed by you got engraved in my emotional chronicle, I often read it, they instilled your presence in my life. I realized I had fallen in love with your thoughts". I added

Time had stopped moving. Ayesha noticed the glory of my discovery of her in every expression of mine, I was not embarrassed either in sharing it.

Nevertheless, she had sensed my curiosity to know more about her.

I lovingly invited some patience into me, it was much required. But, I could not resist telling her about her death.

"It was in the midst of those riots, I returned to Gujranwala, I could find neither of you; I could only find Khushal Singh, living in a dismal state. I discussed with him the possibility of searching for you and your parents in nearby places, requested him to come with me, convincing him to accompany me felt like a struggle. He kept quiet for sometime and finally shared the stark reality". I paused for a moment and continued

"First, it was him but gradually all others in the locality persuaded me to accept the truth and requested me to go back to Amritsar"

All was evident. I could clearly decipher her expression. It began with a shade of sadness and grew into a state where she was being chased by some miserable moments, a dense emotion of discontent was slowly giving way to the dampness in her eyes. But this emotion could not sustain for long, there was a sudden reversal to an expression of gratitude, which she owed, either to god or to someone godly.

My honest narration had not taken her by surpirse either.

My emotions were overwhelming too; I could not control myself from observing her expressions. Those were not just aligned to a sense of sadness but some peculiar sentiments she still lived with. My conversation intuitively indicated my inquisitiveness of her journey from Gujranwala to Fatehpur.

She sat in silence.

I was suddenly reminded of the fact that she could write. With huge hesitation, I extended a piece of paper to her.

Just then Abdul Razzaq approached us.

"Ayesha, here is the man we often heard of, he is the one who can teach us how to listen to the Mother Earth and he has promised me that he will do so".

"Would you teach us today?" he asked me

"Sure, but could I come over tomorrow morning" I sought their permission. Ayesha gauged my intention of seeking a reason to come again the next day.

"Why not?" he responded.

The next morning, both Ayesha and Abdul Razzaq stood listening to me.

"Our bodies are nothing but made up of all these earthen elements, following the laws of this very earth, the changes we cause to this earth brings about the changes in our bodies.

Benazir Patil

A continuous transformation emerging from the law of cause and effect keeps working on us". I explained

"I understand what you are saying but I am not clear about the reference". He said.

"Have you ever spent time with a master of a particular subject? Very soon you realize that your insight is growing rapidly with the interactions you have with that master, similar realization emerges when you spend time with the nature, you learn to understand more from it. I have been talking to Mother Earth since the time I was seven and it feels like she has been the greatest giver of understanding to me than anybody else in this universe." I responded

"What makes you say that?" He asked.

"It is inexplicable, it is an insight that sips into my being, a wisdom, that enters my consciousness, which can be felt and understood by me alone, what exists within me is enough to guide me in my next passage, that is the sheer uniqueness we achieve when we gain wisdom from the masters around us."

"Who are the other masters you have interacted with?"

"Not just me, all of us do, unknowingly we interact with the almighty too, unknowingly, because we hardly allow ourselves to talk with him as we are perpetually engaged in complaining to him rather than counting the blessings bestowed on us. Children are the greatest masters, their naïve perceptions converse a treasure of awareness but our larger than life self-images do not allow us to acknowledge it".

Despite listening to me keenly, Abdul Razzaq's eyes continued to observe Ayesha's expressions. He wondered if there was anything distinct about it.

"You seem to be deeply affected". I suddenly asked Abdul Razzaq, something had tempted me to ask him.

"Yes, indeed, your words are true, they tell us the reality of our lives, what amazes me is the reaction I am witnessing on Ayesha's face, it is indeed strange that in last so many years it is for the first time she is reacting like this." said Abdul Razzaq with a trace of joy.

"You mean last fourteen years?" I questioned.

"Aaa, yes." he responded with an utter shock and looked at me with sheer surprise.

I too realized the folly I had made, how was he to understand my knowledge about Ayesha.

"I need to take your leave, do come again, your talks are indeed mesmerizing, see you soon." He abruptly closed the conversation and walked out

I continued to observe Ayesha for some time and took her leave, with a promise to come back the next day.

The evening was approaching, the twilight encircling its arms around me.

As I was about to walk out of the premises, I sensed a touch on my shoulder. It was none other than Abdul Razzaq, his questioning eyes and curious sensitivity had made him wordless. I looked at him with complete calmness, I thought, it was best that I spoke myself.

"I understand you want to know about the fourteen years, it is strange but true, it was exactly fourteen years ago I had

Benazir Patil

met with Ayesha, I know that there is no one here who can be a witness to my statement. Ayesha herself is the lone witness."

I waited again for his questions, he seemed to have felt little relaxed, but was still unable to express anything. Just then we experienced the light of the lamps that had been lit in the campus.

"The lamps have been lit before the last rays of the sun disappeared, Zeba always said, lighting the lamps well before the end of the day and closing a little after the daybreak ensures continuity of light." I said with a pleasant smile.

I took his leave.

48

Those few days were like dark clouds, which neither thundered nor produced any rains. While, my ears heard the most delightful thoughts and my eyes observed a tireless enthusiasm in her entire being, my mind witnessed a severe sadness buried somewhere.

For two days I had seen her immersed into deep thoughts that had refrained her from much interaction with anyone.

I almost accused myself of disturbing her smile.

Dressed in the garment of simplicity, peace was her closest ally. The weary expressions of the faces that entered the *ashram* were done away with as soon as they mingled with her compassionate semblance.

Questions mounted on my mind, surprisingly, my conversation with Mother Earth added more confusion, because she endlessly conveyed about the healing Ayesha needed.

I decided to talk to Ayesha with complete fearlessness and affection. I quietly transmitted my thoughts, I was prepared to envelope her soul with mine, to embrace all her ghostly and delightful dreams and to rescue her from the raging waves she was drifting with.

She gazed at me, as if asking me to hear all that she was unable to recite. Behind a humble and honest affection for the humanity stood a misery concocted with tremendous bitterness that strove her in helping others erase their hardships.

"You surely cannot be bothered of your future! Your present is filled with the spirit of service and I have witnessed your past, which had nothing but magical words, deep thoughts and adorable acts. Your soul is determined to shield the mankind from ignorance; you are here to narrate the kind acts of humanity and rehearse the songs of mercy. But I see a chasm between all of these, a chasm, undiscovered, that has led you to this weariness". I said to her.

There was no response.

Where was I and what was I talking, I asked myself.

I felt as if I stood at the door of an unforeseen beginning, like a blind man who was lost in the alleys of his path but had delightfully found his destiny after traversing much and struggling profusely. As usual Mother Earth had come to my rescue, she revealed to me about love that was eternal, which was never to perish. Along with the secret of reunion, she ardently whispered to me about the unfinished conversation I was to conclude with Ayesha.

Though I was not to ask anything, the visions of unfolding the complicated knots of her mind were getting stronger with every passing day.

"Ayesha, permit me to understand the truth of your condition!" I exclaimed

"Permit me to share my experience too, time is not real, I have experienced this often and often again. And if time is not real, then the gap which seems to be between the world and the eternity, between suffering and blissfulness, between evil and good, is also a deception".

"I want to understand, what you are living with is the truth or the deception?"

"Come with me, let me make you hear the Mother Earth"

"Let your forehead touch the Earth, and let it absorb all that she is singing for you; it is time you feel her blessings." I sat down, knelt and prostrated, while she sat next to me, I signalled her to do the same.

Keen to understand, she followed me obediently without any questions.

After a while, I sat up, watching her intently listening to the Mother Earth.

In some time she sat up, closed her eyes and prostrated once again, without paying any heed to my attentiveness to her.

For long she continued to listen and sat up again. Her face filled with a massive expression of turmoil. My mute gaze refrained from being an enquirer.

Something was rousing impulsively in her being. Mother Earth had re-established what she had experienced before. Entrapped by the burden of suffering, she clung to sinking pillars of mindfulness. Her expressions loudly declared of apathy towards something. She covered her face with her hands as if she was shielding her eyes from someone, as if she was being ridiculed by the mob in the middle of the road.

"Ayesha means the one who is alive! The mother of believers! I exclaimed

"Is not the most beautiful remembrance in our lives that of the mother and the most wonderful call is for the mother?

She is everything, our consolation in sorrow, our hope in misery, our strength in weakness and our will in forgiveness"

She looked at me with a sense of shock; my words had unearthed something unknown and unfamiliar.

I continued talking what I felt.

"You are *Durga*, the invincible; *Manah*, the mind; *Nitya*, the eternal one; *Satya*, the truth; *Yati*, the ascetic; *Ananta*, the infinite; and *Kshama*, the forgiving. You are the one with seven *Shaktis*"

"Forgiving!" she exclaimed with tears in her eyes

"No Khuda, I am not, I am certainly not!" This time it was a shriek.

But, I wasn't taken aback, this was impending. The assertion of her words was indeed relieving, but calling my name was most comforting, I felt christened, it was ceremonial!

"It is a grudge, and a lot of malice"

"It is not about that terror or the fire or those tragic deaths, it is me, myself"

I unknowingly held her hand and let her talk. She was trembling with distress. She shared about the most humiliating moments and the deepest wounds.

"I dreaded what he had done to me, I ran without realizing where I was heading, having escaped from one nightmare, I stood in front of the next, this time it were four of them together, I cried heavily and the cry itself instilled some weird energy in me, by the time, I realized what I was doing I seemed to have ran incessantly and had jumped into the well. The well, sans of water, was filled with a heap of women, some of them dead and some of them still dying. I realized I was also to die soon. Breathing the stink of decayed human flesh, with complete darkness, I soon lost my consciousness. Few hours later, I felt as if my body was being dragged by two hands. That is the end of my memory." she said

I was quietly listening to her. Khushal Singh had narrated the same, he had had confusion about her death; according to him, it was either the well or the fire.

"Hours later, I regained consciousness, I lay there in the midst of wounded and the dead, it was a hospital like place.

The next day, when I was being asked about my whereabouts, I heard an unknown voice responding on my behalf. "She is my daughter, Ayesha, we would be travelling back to Fatehpur tomorrow". I said nothing at all to interrupt the old man. The old man and his wife helped me search for my father and found that he had died in the fire that was lit in our house that night and my mother too had jumped into the well and had got lost into the heap of dead bodies. The old couple from Fathepur had lost their children in the havoc, the dead body of their daughter Ayesha lay beside me as she was being identified. Clueless about who I was, they pleaded for my love"

"I remained as quiet as you were in those days, I thought, the strange quietness inside me was a phase I will survive and overcome, but little did I know that I had lost the art, the urge and the need to speak to anyone, the speechlessness continued till it became a part of my everyday life. I realized there were many who had been through the same fate as mine, and my struggle to bring them some solace began. They all call me "Ayesha".

Benazir Patil

"While breathing his last, my father asked me to extend my love to those who lived in pain of humiliation" Tears rolled down steadily from her eyes.

"Earth-shattering it was! Moving out of Gujranwala was like crossing over dead bodies, people had perished like decayed leaves. Grief and humiliation had become friends of those who had survived the terror. Some days later, I was told that eleven hundred dead bodies were gradually removed from the same well from where I was dragged out. I was aghast, I was one of the few survivors amongst all of those"

That disdainful experience had robbed her of her faith in the humanity.

In the midst of all the narration, she glanced at me with her kind eyes, which had a strange delight in them despite all the pain. I said nothing, I did not need to, and her patience was rewarded by cheerful energies that my heart was letting out to her.

She prostrated to the Mother Earth, but this time she stretched her hands out to gift her something ardently. Her pale face with shades of sorrow was now filled with tears of gratitude. Her soul wanted to embrace something she had been running away from in last so many years. She lifted her head and cried again.

"Lord almighty!

> "Why didn't I comprehend your purpose of keeping me alive?"
> "Why didn't I envisage my existence as fulfilment of my *karma*?"
> "Why didn't I realize your strength of instilling strength inside me?"

"Why did I assume that you were strong and I was weak, you were powerful and I was helpless, that you had love within you and you seized all the love that filled my heart?"

"Why did I think that by giving me a new life you had planted the seeds of death in my soul?"

"Why did I believe that by exposing to the wounds of others you enhanced my anguish?"

"Why did I meditate on the impediments crafted by you and refused to see the path that radiated affection?"

She turned towards me and exclaimed with a sense of ecstasy.

"See these eyes and see these hands, these hands have borne and transmitted the strength to others to live with virtue and to fight the deadly struggle of life with truth and love. See this soul, once upon a time this conveyed the lessons of suffering and joy, the explanation of god's purpose in giving plight. See this heart, this boasted of converting the ugly and the horrible into beauty and wonder. All the silence within converted the atmosphere of despair to a wave of illumination. But, despite all this Khuda, what is it that I have not been able to change? What is it that I am unable to deal with? What is that one thing that my heart could not embrace?"

"Forgiveness! I could not embrace!"

"Torturers! I could never forgive!"

I wondered, had it not been for me, the evidence of Ayesha's past would have got buried forever, but I saved myself from this self-regarding myth. Thick layers of tales and legend would have got collected around her name, translating her words into myriad philosophies, some in agreement with the ones narrated by the older prophets and some challenging their very basics.

"Thank you, for bringing me back to the Mother Earth!" She said to me with deep sense of gratitude.

"People sin, and the nature of their deeds is acknowledged by their conscience alone, many of them sin only to realize there own inabilities and incapacities to measure strength but they forget that human life is transitory and so are there emotions, one moment they rejoice and the other they regret. That is why it is said, that when life hammers you, rejoice not in the pain of the strike but in the depth of its effect". I said to Ayesha

Those few moments had rejuvenated her, her dispute with her fate had ended, her suffering had vanished. Her face radiated the cheerfulness of the realization she had accomplished.

49

The aroma of *Khichdi* drove me to the days of silence, to Gujranwala, to the moments of admiration for Shivani. It was not unlikely of me to get swayed into the memories that pulled me back in time. I fell into a trance, but soon Ayesha's words drew me to the real moments I was into with her.

"Once, the Buddha was sitting under a tree talking to his disciples when a man came and spit on his face. He wiped it off, and he asked the man, 'What next? What do you want to say to me?' The man was a little puzzled because he himself never expected that when you spit on somebody's face, he would ask this. He had no such experience in his past. He had insulted people and they had become angry and they had reacted. Or if they were cowards and weaklings, they had smiled, trying to bribe the man. But the Buddha was like neither, he was not angry nor in any way offended, nor in any way cowardly. But just matter-of-factly he said,

"What next?" There was no reaction on his part.

This had aroused huge anger amongst Buddha's disciples. His closest disciple, Ananda, said, "This is too much, and we cannot tolerate it. He has to be punished for it. Otherwise everybody will start doing things like this."

The Buddha said, "You keep silent. He has not offended me at all; it is you who are offending me. He is new, a stranger. He must have heard from people something about me, that this man is an atheist, a dangerous man who is throwing people off their track, a revolutionary, and a deceitful creature. And he may have formed some idea, a notion of me. He has not spit on me; he has spit on his notion. He has spit on his idea of me because he does not know me at all, so how can he spit on me?

"If you think on it deeply," Buddha said, "he has spit on his own mind. I am not part of it, and I can see that this poor man must have something else to say because this is a way of saying something. Spitting is a way of saying something. There are moments when you feel that language is impotent: in deep love, in intense anger, in hate and in prayer. There are intense moments when language is impotent. Then you have to do something. When you are angry, intensely angry, you hit the person, you spit on him, you are saying something. I can understand him. He may definitely have something more to say, that's why I asked him, "What next?" I am more offended by you because you know me, and you have lived for years with me, and still you react over such things."

The man had left from there, he returned home, completely puzzled and confused. He could not sleep the whole night. Repeatedly, he was haunted by the experience. He could not explain to himself, what had happened. He was trembling all over and perspiring. He had never come across such a man; he capsized his whole mind, his whole past.

The next morning he was back there. He threw himself at the Buddha's feet. The Buddha asked him again, "What next? This, too, is a way of saying something that cannot be said in language. When you come and touch my feet, you are saying something that cannot be said ordinarily, for which all words are a little narrow; it cannot be contained in them." Buddha said, "Look, Ananda, this man is again here, he is saying something. This man is a man of deep emotions."

The man looked at the Buddha and said, "Forgive me for what I did yesterday."

Benazir Patil

Buddha said, "Forgive? But I am not the same man to whom you did it. The Ganges goes on flowing; it is never the same Ganges again. Every man is a river. The man you spit upon is no longer here. I look just like him, but I am not the same, much has happened in these twenty-four hours! The river has flowed so much. So I cannot forgive you because I have no grudge against you."

"And you also are new. I can see you are not the same man who came yesterday because that man was angry and he spit, whereas you are bowing at my feet, touching my feet. How can you be the same man? You are not the same man, so let us forget about it. Those two people, the man who spit and the man on whom he spit, both are no more. Come closer. Let us talk of something else."

Ayesha paused after narrating the story.

After everybody had left, she looked at me, for a long time, we both said nothing.

"Khuda, my sunken state had blocked my mind, I have now found my peace, the peace of forgiveness that always lay within me". Overpowered by her own sentiments she finally expressed.

All these years, I had learned to live by *Ketaab-e-Hayaat*, some of it I understood and some I didn't. But it had been almost a year now, I had not unwrapped that yellow satin cloth, I did not need to. Ironically though, the almighty, the infinite entity, has always been expressed in finite terms; finite forms and finite rules locked and bundled up into the books and scriptures that often remain unread, seated on our shelves.

For me, Ayesha was a symbol of this infinity, an infinity that was infinitely escalating every moment to a height I could not measure up to, not that I wanted to; living in awe of her was an ever-longing bliss.

Benazir Patil

Glossary

- *Ab-e-Hayaat:* The fountain of life
- *Ab-e-Zamzam:* Water of 'Zamzam', the sacred well near Kaabah
- *Abyad:* White, bright, radiant and pure
- *Ajil-e-shirin:* A mixture of nuts, dry-fruits and sweets
- *Al-Kabeer:* One of Allah's 99 names, meaning 'The Greatest'
- *Ashram:* A monastery or a habitat that provides accommodation for destitute people
- *Atman:* Inner self or soul
- *Azaan:* A call to prayer/worship called out by a Muezzin from the mosque five times a day
- *Beti:* Term for daughter in Hindi
- *Bhai:* Term for brother in Hindi
- *Dakil:* A thread or a tress fastened on a sacred place, object, the railing around a saint's tomb, grave or a tree considered sacred, in order to obtain a desired benefit
- *Darakht-e-Morad:* The sacred tree which could fulfil the desires and wishes
- *Dasht-e-Kavir:* the Great Salt Desert, lying in the middle of the Iranian plateau is the world's 23rd largest desert
- *Dasht-e-Lut:* Referred as 'Desert of Emptiness' is a large salt desert in south-eastern Kerman Iran and is the world's 25th largest desert
- *Dervish:* A religious mendicant, a member of a Muslim (specifically Sufi) religious order who has taken vows of poverty and austerity.
- *Gayatri:* A goddess seated on red-lotus, signifying wealth, considered to be the mother of all, an aspect of goddesses Saraswati, Parvati and Lakshmi, all three in one form. Also a personification of the hymn 'Gayatri Mantra'
- *Isa:* An Arabic name corresponding to Jesus in English, mentioned in the Quran
- *Jap Ji:* A universal sacred hymn about God composed by Guru Nanak Dev Ji, the founder of the Sikh faith.
- *Kaabah:* A cuboid building at the centre of Islam's most sacred mosque, Al-Masjid al-Haram, in Mecca, Saudi Arabia.
- *Karshvar:* Zones, regions or divisions the world is divided into
- *Ketaab-e-Hayaat:* Book of life
- *Khichdi:* A South Asian preparation made from rice and lentils (dal)
- *Korsi:* A type of low table with a heater underneath it, and blankets thrown over it. A traditional furniture of Iranian culture popularly used for family or other gatherings during meals and special events

- *Musa: An Arabic name corresponding to Moses in English, mentioned in the Quran*
- *Nirvana: Meaning "to extinguish", a concept in Buddhism that refers to a state of mind filled with peace and bliss, a state in which the fires of desire, aversion, and delusion have been finally extinguished*
- *Nowroz: Meaning "New Day", is the first day on the Iranian calendar*
- *Ojas: Meaning "vigor", is one of the essential ingredients of the body that builds life-force as per the principles of Ayurveda*
- *Parwaaz: The first flight of a bird*
- *Pranayama: A science of regulation of breathing*
- *Prithvi Namaskar: Saluting the earth by paying obeisance to her*
- *Pauri: A stanza*
- *Qiblah: Direction that is faced during salat/namaaz/prayers*
- *Rusari: A type of head-scarf worn by Iranian Women*
- *Sapta-rishis: Seven Sages mentioned in the Vedas, also are considered to be a group of stars*
- *Shab-e-Yalda: Meaning "Night of Birth", is the Persian winter solstice celebration, celebrated on the Northern Hemisphere's longest night of the year on or around December 20 or 21 each year.*
- *Shakti: Cosmic energy, the divine power of Goddess Durga*
- *Simorgh: a benevolent, mythical flying creature, found in all periods of Greater Iranian art and literature as a bird that is thought to possess the knowledge of all the ages and was considered to purify the land and waters and hence bestow fertility.*
- *Tasawwuf: A theological path of Sufis with a belief system of man's relationship with god*
- *Uru-Salim: Another name for Jerusalem, means 'city of peace'*
- *Veda: Meaning "knowledge" is a large body of sacred texts originating in ancient India constituting the oldest layer of Sanskrit literature and the earliest literary record of Indo-Aryan civilization.*
- *Vohu Manah: The Avestan language term for a Zoroastrian concept, generally translated as "Good Purpose" or "Good Mind", referring to the good moral state of mind that enables an individual to accomplish his duties.*
- *Vorukasha: A heavenly sea in Zoroastrian mythology. It is a world-ocean which surrounds the seven continents and was created by Ahura Mazda and sent down to the earth to cleanse the world of all its pollution*
- *Wiccans: Followers of a modern pagan religion called Wicca*
- *Zarthosht: An Indian/Persian name corresponding to Zoroaster and Zarathustra*
- *Ziggurat: A temple tower of the ancient Assyrians and Babylonians, having the form of a terraced pyramid of successively receding stories.*

Benazir Patil

About the Author

Benazir, born in India, is a development specialist by profession and has been working with several social development organizations both in India and internationally. Through her work she has directly touched the lives of the discriminated and disadvantaged. She holds a PhD in Public Health Policy, and has authored many academic books.

This is her first work of fiction.